# Small Churches
# Are Beautiful

# Small Churches are Beautiful

*Edited by*

## Jackson W. Carroll

*1817*

Published in San Francisco by
**HARPER & ROW, PUBLISHERS**

New York, Hagerstown, San Francisco, London

FIRST EDITION

*Designed by Eve Callahan*

---

**Library of Congress Cataloging in Publication Data**

Main entry under title:
Small churches are beautiful.

    Includes bibliographical references.
    1. Small churches—Addresses, essays, lectures.
I. Carroll, Jackson W.
BV637.8.S62  1977    261    76–62948
ISBN 0–06–061319–X

---

77 78 79 80 81 10 9 8 7 6 5 4 3 2 1

# Contents

# List of Contributors

JEFFERY S. ATWATER: Pastor of Lyme Town Ministry, Lyme, New Hampshire.

JACKSON W. CARROLL: Coordinator of Research in the Church and Ministry Program, Hartford Seminary Foundation, Hartford, Connecticut.

RICHARD E. COLBY: Program Facilitator of the Shared Ministry Project, Episcopal Diocese of Maine, Portland, Maine.

THEODORE H. ERICKSON: Planning Associate for the United Church Board for Homeland Ministries (United Church of Christ), New York, New York.

JAMES C. FENHAGEN: Director and Coordinator for Professional Development of the Church and Ministry Program, Hartford Seminary Foundation, Hartford, Connecticut.

JAMES W. FRASER: Minister of Education, Church of the Covenant, Boston, Massachusetts, and Research Fellow, Auburn Theological Seminary, New York, New York.

DOUGLAS W. JOHNSON: Executive Vice-President of the Institute for Church Development, Ridgewood, New Jersey.

ROBERT W. LYNN: Vice-President for Religion, The Lilly Endowment, Incorporated, Indianapolis, Indiana.

ARTHUR C. TENNIES: Pastor of the Tuscarora United Presbyterian Church and the Mount Morris United Church, Mount Morris, New York.

DOUGLAS A. WALRATH: Secretary for Regional Services and Coordinator, Northeastern Regional Center, Reformed Church in America, Schenectady, New York.

ALAN K. WALTZ: Assistant General Secretary for Research, General Council on Ministries, United Methodist Church, Dayton, Ohio.

CHARITY WAYMOUTH: Senior Research Scientist, Jackson Laboratories, Bar Harbor, Maine.

ROBERT L. WILSON: Research Professor of Church and Society, Divinity School of Duke University, Durham, North Carolina.

# Introduction

*Jackson W. Carroll*

In his collection of essays, *Small Is Beautiful: Economics As If People Mattered*, E. F. Schumacher[1] has challenged some basic assumptions that have guided Western economic and social development: bigger is better; quality is measured by quantity; success is to be equated with size. In place of such assumptions, he proposes an economy and a society in which people matter and in which the possibilities for creativity and altruism are enhanced by human-scale institutions and communities. Schumacher's book is not a utopian fantasy; it is a serious proposal for a new direction. His concern seems to be shared by more and more people. Recent migration trends in the United States have suggested to some analysts a major change in Americans' expectations. Pollster Louis Harris has said that "most Americans don't want more quantity of anything, but more quality in what they've got" (quoted in *Time*, 15 March 1976). I doubt that most Americans would share all aspects of Schumacher's program; nevertheless, the "small is beautiful" theme seems to be contagious.

This book is an effort to affirm a slight variant of that theme—small *can be* beautiful—in relation to the church. More specifically, it is about new possibilities open to small churches to celebrate their smallness as a positive attribute and to develop their potential as vital, caring communities of faith.

Small churches are defined here, somewhat arbitrarily, as churches with memberships of two hundred persons or less. Over 50 percent of the congregations in most major Protestant churches are covered by this definition. In the United Presbyterian Church the figure is 52 percent. The United Church of Christ has 51 percent. The proportion of churches with two hundred members or less increases to 62 percent for both the United Methodist Church and the Disciples of Christ, and in the Presbyterian Church U.S., 72 percent of the churches have fewer than two hundred fifty members. Similar figures were not available for the Episcopal church, but a study of 1967–68 statistics by James Lowery[2] estimated that approximately 62 percent of Episcopal churches were below the line of economic viability ($20,000 annual budget), reflecting a probable adult membership of two hundred or less. Only the Southern Baptists, American Lutheran Church, and Lutheran Church in America, among major Protestant denominations, reported fewer than 50 percent of their churches in the two-hundred-member category, and their figures were all over 40 percent. No figures are available for Roman Catholics, nor do we have figures from other Protestant denominations, but nothing suggests that the situation would be very different among these groups.[3]

If small is beautiful, these churches are an opportunity and a challenge to develop communities that faithfully and effectively engage in the continuing ministry and mission of Jesus Christ in ways appropriate to their size, resources, and setting. What constitutes faithful and effective ministry and mission in a large congregation is not necessarily the appropriate model for small churches. Just as the Word became flesh in a *particular* person, a *particular* place, and a *particular* time and culture, the communities of faith that participate in the continuing ministry of the Word experience the particularities of their time, place, and size.

To be sure, small churches, like large ones, are called to celebrate and proclaim God's gracious Word—Jesus Christ, to nurture persons and support their personal and spiritual development, to foster community and expressions of caring among their members, and to engage in Christ's mission in the world. These core functions of ministry and mission are the same for all churches regardless of size, but the forms in which they are expressed—organizational structures and programs—vary considerably. Congregational size, resources, and setting are major factors affecting the variation.

Small churches, by virtue of their size, have unique opportunities for vital functioning in some areas that are not normally open to larger churches. The chapters that follow suggest some of these opportunities for intimacy, caring, and support; opportunities for the development of mutual ministry of clergy and laity; opportunities for significant intergenerational experiences; and opportunities for mission in the community, especially in rural and small communities where churches have considerable credibility and strength to promote needed changes.

Unfortunately these and other opportunities that small size offers are often missed. A serious problem is that neither small-church members nor denominational leaders have always believed in these possibilities. Many small churches have perceived themselves as mediocre and nonviable, and these negative images have often become self-fulfilling prophecies. Denominational leaders, viewing small churches as drains on scarce denominational resources, have sought to merge, yoke, or cluster them into larger and, presumably, more effective units. Failing this, they have closed them in large numbers over the years.

Many small churches are mediocre and nonviable as currently functioning. This should be acknowledged in all candor and honesty. Out of a sense of denominational stewardship, some may need to be closed. If bigger does not always mean better, neither is small always beautiful.

The chapters that follow, while reflecting the particular con-

cerns and experiences of the authors, are nevertheless tied together by a shared perspective and some common themes. These
were identified and given shape through meetings and cor-
respondence over several months. Most of the authors and others
who served as consultants came together initially at a meeting at
the Hartford Seminary Foundation, Hartford, Connecticut, in
June 1975. Their purpose was to identify basic issues facing small
congregations and to develop a strategy for addressing them.
Several of those present agreed to prepare working papers for a
symposium on small congregations. Others, not present at the
consultation, were provided notes from the meeting and invited
to prepare papers.

These papers, including three plenary addresses and three
video-taped case studies of small congregations, became the sub-
stantive basis for the symposium held in Hartford in January 1976
when there was considerable discussion and feedback from a
large number of participants. The authors and those making
plenary addresses then revised their papers to make up the chapters of this book. A grant by the Lilly Endowment made possible
both the research and the symposium.

Because we believe it to be a helpful perspective for understanding small churches, we have drawn heavily on what might
be called a social systems view. We look at the church in its
organization or incarnate life as a social system of interdependent
parts, not unlike Paul's perspective on the church in 1 Corinthians
12. Thus we examine such elements of the church's life as its
image of itself, its ordained and lay leadership, its program and
resources, and its structure. These are the internal elements of the
church system. The church as a system, however, exists in a context that both affects and is affected by it. Here we deal with
aspects of both the larger social and cultural environment of
small churches—the national scene—and how the local community affects church functioning. Additionally, we consider the
denomination and its role relative to the small church. Finally, we
view the church as existing in a temporal flow, moving from a

past that continues to exert its influence on the present, toward a future which shapes the present as it is anticipated in planning and action.

A number of common themes began to emerge as we worked together and individually on our assignments. First, categories used in analyzing, understanding, and planning must be appropriate to the small church. In our society, we have been so strongly affected (afflicted?) by the worship of size, rationality, and efficiency that it is difficult not to draw on this "trinity" in considering the small church. During the symposium, for example, several persons noted that the current emphasis on clustering small churches into cooperative parishes—however helpful in many cases—is really the attempt to help small churches experience the benefits enjoyed by large churches having multiple staffs and diverse programs. The assumption is that these benefits are intrinsically worthwhile and needed by all churches, regardless of size. It is difficult to eliminate such assumptions from our thinking, but we have attempted to be conscious of this in our work.

A second theme, flowing in part from the first, is that images small churches hold of themselves and their situation are crucial to the way they function. A chapter by Arthur Tennies focuses on this theme, and it is also taken up by several of the other authors. It is an acknowledgment of the considerable wisdom in the dictum: "If men define situations as real, they are real in their consequences."[4] Small churches need not define themselves as second class by virtue of their size.

A third theme, already mentioned, is that considerable opportunities are open to small churches more or less naturally as a result of their size. To enable small congregations to identify these opportunities and move toward meeting them is an important task.

A fourth common theme is that form follows function. Small churches have often been the victims of polity requirements and programs that were designed with medium to large churches in mind and of structural schemes imposed by the denomination in cookie-cutter fashion with little awareness of local situations and needs. We believe that programs and structures for small churches should grow out of the congregation's understanding of what it means to be faithful to Christ's mission in its own local situation.

Finally, there runs throughout the chapters an emphasis on mutuality. Denominations, especially middle judicatories, have an important role relative to congregations that is best fulfilled when the integrity of the church is respected and when assessment and envisioning for the future is shared. Neither heavy-handed nor subtle paternalism is appropriate. Mutuality of ministry between laity and clergy is also given emphasis in a number of chapters; it is not paternalistic clergy and dependent laity that are needed, but recognition and support of the gifts and calling each of the other. While this need for mutuality is not peculiar to small congregations, we believe it is a key element in their renewal.

The perspective on the church as a social system and these several common themes undergird this work through which we hope to raise new possibilities for small churches.

## NOTES

1. E. F. Schumacher, *Small Is Beautiful: Economics As If People Mattered* (New York: Harper & Row, 1973).

2. James L. Lowery, Jr., *Peers, Tents, and Owls, Some Solutions to Problems of Clergy Today* (New York: Morehouse-Barlow, 1973).

3. Statistics reported for the denominations (other than Episcopal) are for the following years: United Presbyterian, 1974; United Church of Christ, 1973; United Methodist, 1969; Disciples of Christ, 1974; Presbyterian U.S., 1968; Southern Baptist, 1974; and Lutheran Churches, 1975. Appreciation is expressed to Earl D. C. Brewer, who initially collected most of the statistics, and to the denominational statisticians who made them available.

4. See Lewis A. Coser and Bernard Rosenberg, eds., *Sociological Theory* (New York: Macmillan, 1957), pp. 231–35.

# Small Churches
# Are Beautiful

# 1

# Images of the Small Church in American History

*Robert W. Lynn and James W. Fraser*

If you remember the 1930s, you may recall the story of the airplane pilot who came to be known as "Wrong Way Corrigan." Although his flight plans called for a trip from New York City to the West Coast, Corrigan took off in the opposite direction and landed in Europe. Like Corrigan, we are taking off in the wrong direction. Instead of addressing ourselves directly to the topic of the small church's past, we would like first to examine its future as it appeared to some of our most vocal forebearers. Real small churches, cutting across theological, class, and urban-rural lines, have embodied a great variety of more- and less-faithful communities of Christians, but the dominant image of the small church, among novelists and church planners, has been less diverse.

In 1887 Edward Bellamy wrote what became, along with *Uncle Tom's Cabin* and *Ben Hur*, one of the most popular novels of the second half of the nineteenth century. Though now obscure, *Looking Backward* still gives some sense of what a reform-minded preacher's son from Connecticut thought the twentieth century held for the small congregation.

The plot is simple. A thirty-year-old man falls asleep in 1887, only to wake up in Rip Van Winkle style, in the year 2000. He is astonished to find a "new" and "beautiful" American society around him, an egalitarian society free of class conflict and the subordination of women, and characterized by high productivity, ample leisure, and material comfort for all. He is glad to see that "there were no lawyers," but when he asks if a revolution had taken place in the churches, he learns the society still "had Sundays and the churches."

Now, "as to hearing a sermon today," his "twentieth-century" host explains, "If you wish to do so, you could either go to church or hear it here at home."

"How am I to hear it if I stay at home?"

"Simply by accompanying us to the music room at the proper hour and selecting an easy chair."

(Remember, this is 1887 . . . no radio, no television, of course.) His host goes on:

> There are some who still prefer to hear sermons in church, but most of our preaching, like our musical performances, is not in public, but delivered rather in acoustically secured chambers connected by wire with subscribers' houses. If you prefer to go to a church, I shall be glad to accompany you, but I really don't believe that you are likely to hear anywhere a better discourse than you will at home. I see by the paper that Mr. Barton is to preach this morning, and he preaches only by telephone, and to audiences often reaching 150,000.[1]

There is no place in Bellamy's vision for any church of the kind we are talking about in this book. Indeed, he probably would have been surprised—and disappointed—that such antiquated institutions would still be with us at all, three-quarters of the way through the twentieth century.

In a 1944 *Christian Century* article, a Congregational minister from Wisconsin stood on tiptoe, so to speak, to view life beyond World War II. Ironically, he focused on 1984, as did George Orwell a mere five years later when he wrote his anti-utopian novel *1984.*

According to the author, Clarence Seidenspinner, there is no room in our future for the small congregation. In his account, Sunday morning comes, and you venture from your hotel room to find a church. Although there are still a few old Gothic and Romanesque buildings around, the structure that catches your eye is new. It is obviously a church even though it occupies a full block and bears little resemblance to the cathedrals of yesterday. You enter and pass through the portals of the church, which incidentally stands twenty stories high, to sit in the nave where thousands of people are gathered. Worshippers have been taking their places to participate in the service. The prelude is a complex, thrilling experience—a symphony.

No ordinary sermons in the church of 1984! When a pastor preaches on religious and nervous tensions, he calls upon the physicians, psychiatrists, and social workers in the congregation to plan the sermon with him. Likewise, when he preaches on God in nature, he calls on the chemists, biologists, and engineers.

Following worship and after lunch in the coffee shop in the lobby, you take an elevator to the second-floor offices, a massive suite that would put the Interchurch Center in New York City to shame. The fifth floor contains the educational rooms; books, maps, sound projectors, recordings, pictures, and competent teachers make possible serious study in Christian living. I won't take you beyond the fifth floor, but the minister from Wisconsin leads his readers to the twentieth floor on his imaginary tour of the Protestant American church of the future.

When you return to your hotel room, especially if you are an outlander, you may say, "This is wonderful, to be sure, and is on a magnificent scale. But even in my own modest community something like this can be done." And then you begin to think and plan:

> Small, struggling, separatistic churches are no longer necessary or right. These groups can be combined to form larger churches. . . . Even in the open country, churches can be combined and fine buildings erected, comparable to our consolidated schools. There will be no need for the one- or two-room country church when buses and cars can take the membership to a thrilling and busy and beautiful consolidated church in which generous and far-reaching fellowship may be enjoyed with a staff of competent leaders.[2]

Such factors as theological diversity and the cultural identity of varying ethnic groups evidently had no place in the new age. This description might have seemed credible to some Protestants in 1944, but fortunately it now looks as if we may not arrive at this particular utopia by 1984 after all.

Perhaps through knowledge of our ancestors' glimpses of tomorrow, we are better equipped to understand how we perceive the present role of the small church and congregation. For all our attempts to ignore them, we still carry these images in our memories. We Americans have always chased the future, and our—perhaps outmoded—dreams of tomorrow reveal much about where we are, what we think, and what we believe today.

Of course, there have been other visions. William Pitts's old song invited nostalgia with its plea:

> O come to the church in the wildwood,
> O come to the church in the dale;
> No spot is so dear to my childhood
> As the little brown church in t'ıe vale.

After the Civil War when novelist Harriet Beecher Stowe turned her attention to celebrating the old virtues of her native New England, she gave the small church a place of honor:

> Going to meeting, in that state of society into which I was born, was as necessary and inevitable a consequence of waking up on Sunday morning as eating one's breakfast. Nobody thought of stay-

ing away,—and for that matter, nobody wanted to stay away. Our weekly life was simple, monotonous, and laborious; and the chance of seeing the whole neighborhood together in their best clothes on Sunday was a thing which, in the dearth of all other sources of amusement, appealed to the idlest and most unscriptural of loafers.[3]

These happy images of small-church life are part of our collective memory, but warm as these remembrances are, they are also nostalgic memories of childhood. They might be acceptable for the past, but when serious people began to plan for the future, quite different images emerged. For most white and many black Protestants in the north and east, especially in those denominations which have long considered themselves mainline, the two scenarios of the future written in 1887 and in 1944 constitute a vote of no confidence in the future of the small congregation. Like Main Street in a small town, a small parish has developed a bad name. The small church might provide a sentimental past, but as a future assignment it seemed more like damnation. Two further fictional examples contrast the reactions of two ministers, one assigned to a small church, the other to a large one.

*The Damnation of Theron Ware* is a typical turn-of-the-century novel about a minister in crisis. Theron Ware was a promising young Methodist preacher living in a small town in upstate New York. When asked to preach the sermon at an annual conference, he developed hopes and aspirations for being appointed to one of the city churches, probably in Utica or Syracuse. But when the new assignments were announced, Theron was sent to a small town, once more damned to provincialism. As he and his wife, depressed and defeated, left the meeting, Mrs. Ware turned to her husband and said:

Why, Theron, they tell me it's a worst place even than we've got now."
"Oh, not at all," he tried to reassure her, "it's a great Irish place, I've heard. Our own church seems to be a good deal run down there. We must build it up again; and the salary *is* better—a little."

But he too was depressed, and they walked on toward their temporary lodging in a silence filled with mutual grief.

Then he tried to comfort her once more. He said, "Come, let us make the best of it, my girl! After all, we are in the hands of the Lord."

"Oh, don't, Theron!" she said to him, "Don't talk to me about the Lord tonight; I can't bear it!"

Theron Ware felt damned to a particularly narrow hell— although novelist Harold Frederic knew there was a much worse hell waiting for Theron as a result of his false sense of superiority to his parishioners.[4]

A more recent spate of novels on handsome clergymen also draw on the bad reputation of the small church. In 1946–48 a variety of novels was published featuring a new literary hero, the pastor of the large congregation or the minister with obvious promise and on his way up. The hero of *The Bishop's Mantle* was a priest:

> At nine o'clock on a bright March morning a young man in his first thirties walked slowly along High Street. He was tall with the shoulders and waist of an athlete. . . . His clothes were distinctly well-tailored and he wore them with an easy nonchalance. A stranger interested enough to hazard a guess might have set him down as a handsome young lawyer, or a business man with his feet well set upon the ladder of success. They would have probably not have surmised that he was a clergyman coming to assume the duties of his first large parish.[5]

Once again, escape for the minister meant a move out of the small town and far from the tiny congregation to "larger fields of service." Why this preoccupation, this obsession, with the large church and the corresponding disdain and condescension for a tiny parish?

This preference is not inevitable, for Americans have not always valued the large church more than the small one. In fact, in the eighteenth century during those decades just before the Revolution, no absolute distinction was made between the large and the small church. New England Congregationalist ministers, for example, did not necessarily move from smaller to larger churches. In fact, they didn't move. A study of the graduates of Yale College from 1702 to 1775 shows that 79 percent of those who were ministers served one parish all their lives. The majority served for more than thirty years, and a mere 7 percent had more than two parishes.[6] In those days, it seems, an individual was called by God to a lifelong commitment to the people of God. Both congregation and minister approached the selection with considerable care, as you might imagine, and sometimes the decision was months in the making.

One minister wrote his fiancée, "The people continue to watch me as narrowly as a mouse is watched by a cat."[7] Because of the likelihood of such intense scrutiny and its ramifications, many ministers chose a small but loving and respectful parish over a larger, wealthier one.

One individual who accepted a position in a parish in Hadlyme, Connecticut, did so despite the size of the small town and its inability to offer him a large salary. A harmonious invitation from the residents and a manifestation of their willingness to support him as pastor influenced his decision.

Another pastor said of his small parish:

> There are more Christians. No sectarians; I believe not one. Comparatively few infidels. The people are peaceable. Not a lawyer in the whole country. Industrious, hospitable; in the habit of being influenced by their minister.[8]

The eighteenth-century New England Congregationalists did not view the successful pastor as one who changed churches. That 7 percent with more than two pastorates consisted of the "ne'er to do wells." The situation was precisely the reverse of today, that is, Congregational pastors of that time looked upon themselves as holding identical offices with identical problems. There were no essential spiritual distinctions between the minister who labored in a small Connecticut hamlet and the pastor of the prominent church in New Haven or Boston.

Of course, distinctions were drawn between people; yet such distinctions were not made on the basis of a church's size but according to a person's "power" as a pastor and a preacher. The man in the small church and the man in the large church were both called by God to their respective parishes, and they were both treated equally. Even when Yale College asked a pastor to be professor of divinity and offered to pay what was then an extravagant amount of money to his parish church in New Milford by way of indemnity, the church would not let the minister go.[9]

From our temporal vantage point, it seems a long time ago that the small and large church were considered of equal importance. What happened between then and now? Among Congregationalists the major change came in the nineteenth century, especially after the War of 1812. By 1815, some thirty-five or forty years after the time we have just been considering, the pattern had begun to reverse itself.

By the time Andrew Jackson became president, it was normal for a pastor to serve three or four churches. A minister became a man on the move who worked his way up the ladder.

By the 1820s and the 1830s, more and more white Protestant ministers were willing to approach their work as a career. The small church became a steppingstone to something bigger and greater. The wealthy parish of this period could raid a poor congregation and not even pay compensation.

Indeed, in the 1830s, the word *profession* began to be applied in a new way. Earlier, the notion of profession was indicated in the word *profess*. A *professor* or a *professional* was one who had something to "profess," one who responded to a "call." After 1820 or 1830, a *professional* was a person who entered a "career," and a successful professional minister found his way from the small church to the large church. All entrances to that career were carefully guarded, but once inside, the professional hoped to travel the normal path leading upward.

The career of Henry Ward Beecher, of that ubiquitous nineteenth-century Beecher clan, is a case in point. Lyman Beecher, a remarkable person in his own right, was the proud father of several of the most unusual children ever to grace the American scene. Harriet Beecher Stowe, of course, wrote *Uncle Tom's Cabin*. Catharine Beecher founded one of the first movements toward the education of women. And Henry, the runt of the lot and in his early years the child showing the least promise, was a minister.

In his career, Henry offered a new model of ministry to Protestantism. After graduating from Lane Theological Seminary, he lived two years in Lawrenceberg, Indiana, twenty miles east of Cincinnati, just long enough for his wife to become acquainted with the poverty and hardship of life in a small town. As soon as possible, the Beechers moved to a larger, more well-to-do parish in Indianapolis, and within seven years they were off to suburban Brooklyn. Brooklyn Heights, then the equivalent of today's fashionable suburbs, was the location Henry Ward Beecher chose to establish one of the great American churches, Plymouth Church. He quickly built up a large following. Soon, ferries called "Beecher Boats" carried people on Sunday mornings from Manhattan to Brooklyn Heights.

Plymouth, imitated and envied by many, set a pace for churches of the last century. Plymouth Church and others like it set the standards, becoming the ideal, the norm. What were Plymouth's attractions? First, it offered something for everyone—worship, education, and entertainment, especially drama, which was acceptable to Protestants who were feeling somewhat guilty about being exposed in the theaters of the day. Plymouth and other large churches produced great music as their form of drama and entertainment.

Second, the huge church provided anonymity and an escape

from the constant surveillance of the small town left behind, an oft-repeated theme of diaries and biographies of nineteenth-century Americans. During the 1800s the issue of where a person could participate without risking judgment was important. The transgressions most often discussed by American Protestants were anger, jealousy, and hatred, the sins accompanying life in close quarters. (When Paul Tillich wanted to develop a twentieth-century definition of sin, he thought not about sin as "closeness" but as "distance.")

Third, the large church provided a relaxed standard of membership. It was much easier to be a full-fledged member of a Congregational church like Plymouth than it was to be a halfway church member a century earlier.

For these and other reasons, the Plymouths, the large churches, became fashionable. To this day they have cast their shadow on the life and destiny of the small church, making it a symbol of failure. The laws of success and growth were immutable: To live was to grow in size; to remain small was to die. Countless contenders after Plymouth sought the title of "largest" and "best." Brooklyn filled with huge churches and soon was called "the city of churches."

Across the country the story was much the same. New frontier churches were quick to claim they were the "largest church west of the Mississippi" or "west of Missouri" or "west of the Rocky Mountains." In part, this preoccupation with size reflected what Daniel Boorstin has called "the booster spirit." Pioneers and missionaries hastened to predict a great future for their institutions. One week after the founder of Denver, Colorado, had set up four cottonwood poles and declared the site of the future city of Denver, he wrote his wife back east, "We expect at least a second Sacramento City, at least."[10]

The Sunday school movement, a great religious development, is an example of how the American spirit of "bigness" affected both large and small Protestant congregation. The genius of the early

Sunday school was its flexibility; it could work with four, forty, or four thousand. At first, no distinctions were made between small or large Sunday schools, but after the Civil War a pervasive concern for expansion, growth, and development penetrated the movement. For instance, John Wanamaker, today remembered for his department stores, was most well known during his lifetime as postmaster general of the United States. But personally he considered his greatest accomplishment to be the founding and superintending of the biggest Sunday school in the world. The 1876 Centennial Exposition in Philadelphia featured for sightseers John Wanamaker's mammoth Sunday school.

Recently *Newsweek* and other magazines have reminded us of the continuing competition of Sunday schools for the title of "who's the largest" and "who's the biggest." Parades and contests have been held, and a congregation in Georgia recently staged a reenactment of a Civil War battle to attract more people on Sunday mornings. Such techniques are not altogether new.

The Sunday school needed a statistician to keep a public record on how rapidly the institution was growing. The problem of record keeping took on an awesome complexity. In the early 1900s, Sunday school record forms would do the IRS justice.

Another innovation of that time which is still with us is the record of attendance posted on the walls of at least Baptist, Methodist, and Presbyterian churches. Two symbols dominated these liturgically bare churches—a clock and a record of attendance, both of which illustrate our forebearers' preoccupation with rate of growth.

In the late nineteenth century big Sunday schools enjoyed notice and prestige, which meant that smaller Sunday schools were left behind. From 1890 on, however, a few people in each generation have complained that small Sunday schools and congregations were being ignored, if not forgotten. But such laments have not been satisfactorily heard or embodied in effective reforms.

Why did the national church bureaucracy persist in its patterns of selective inattention to the small congregation? For one thing, early twentieth-century denominational executives were mostly churchmen who held the values and virtues of those who had "made it." By and large, they left the small congregation early in their careers, lost sight of its particular problems, and so began to establish the larger congregation as the norm. To be sure, the smaller congregation was "rediscovered" from time to time. It almost seems as if every generation "discovers anew" the existence of the small congregation, but that discovery never lasted long. Gradually the ideal of the large church came to be taken for granted. For example, a variety of progressive Protestants wanted to reform, to "improve," the Sunday school. *Reforms* meant initiating a graded lesson plan (which required a fairly large Sunday school), hiring a full-time director of Christian Education, and designing new facilities (which almost always kept problems of the large church in mind).

For the most part, American Protestant leaders forgot the small congregations. The first major effort to understand and appreciate the small congregation came out of the rural church movement in the early decades of this century. Between 1900 and 1920, several trends prompted renewed concern.

First, the federal government awoke to a belated recognition of the needs of rural America. Theodore Roosevelt established a commission to study rural life, and soon the YMCA, the YWCA, and church denominations followed suit.

The book, *The Wisconsin Death Trip*, gives insight into life in small, rural communities. It is the photo-historical portrait of a Wisconsin hamlet suffering through the crises of demoralization caused in those left behind by the migration to the city. The photographs of the local residents tell the story, along with newspaper headlines such as those which appeared in 1898: "Sudden Baby Death," "Sad Insanity," "Small Pox Scare," "Set Fire to Herself," "Suicide—Threat of Old Age," "Factories Running Full

Time," "Grim Death," "Mysterious Disappearance," "Insanity,"
"Hired Hand Suicide," "Infant Death Memorialized."[11]

These were just some of the problems which prompted a new
generation of Protestant leaders to draw attention to the "town and
country" church. As these leaders concentrated upon the difficulties of the small church in the rural territory, they saw the problems of short-term pastorates and poorly paid and ill-equipped
ministers. Above all, though, they focused on competition among
denominations, a problem that particularly haunted and angered
reformers. One such reformer began his book *Empty Churches*,
published more than fifty years ago, with a poignant description:

> Recently, in a cross-roads country church, a minister of the Gos-
> pel, underpaid, somewhat shabby, but eager and inspired, a man
> with a message to give, stood before his congregation to present that
> message. The flame and inspiration in his haggard young face flick-
> ered and died as he looked down at the scanty congregation assem-
> bled before him to hear the Word of God. At a glance he counted
> his hand full of pews, six.
>
> Through a window on one side of the little church he could see
> two other meeting-houses nestling in the curve of the road. Through
> a window on the other side he looked at a third—four country
> churches of four Christian denominations almost identical in doc-
> trine, there within two stones throw of one another.
>
> In three of these churches, including his own, he knew that the
> members of the congregation might be counted upon the fingers of
> each pastor's two hands. The third church was closed down.
>
> In all four of those churches, put together, not one fair-sized
> congregation. In all four, not one pastor paid a salary large enough
> to enable him to live on his income as a minister.[12]

Such a view differs greatly from Harvey Cox's memory of small-
town Pennsylvania in the 1930s:

> For a town with fewer than 2,000 souls we were more than
> amply blessed with churches. We did have two saloons and three
> gasoline stations. We had, however, eight churches. God had not
> only not bypassed Malvern, He had also generously provided a rich,

if somewhat bewildering, variety of ways to approach Him. The tribe had several clans, and although there was sometimes suspicion and sniping among them, there was never intratribal war. Maybe that is why I've always been a pluralist. When you grow up in a town where on a warm Sunday with all the church windows open you can hear gospel hymns being sung and the Mass being chanted at the same moment, pluralism comes easy.[13]

But while Cox may speak effectively for the 1970s, when pluralism and smallness are being rediscovered, this sort of denominationalism was seen as an outrage and a scandalous waste of money to most reformers of previous generations. The pressure was for the consolidated church, and for this the public school provided a model.

The proposed programs for those consolidated churches in rural America resemble, albeit in covert ways, the model of the larger church. Some reformers wanted to take the institutional church out of the city and transpose it to the countryside. They were developing a cutdown version of Henry Ward Beecher's old model.

In retrospect, one can say that the rural-church movement of the early twentieth century, at best, still used the large-church model as the standard for measurement and comparison. The weight of Plymouth, the shadow of our preoccupation and obsession with bigness, dominated even that group. But, whatever its deficiencies, the rural-church movement recognized the reality of life in a small congregation, until the depression slowed its momentum.

For the generation after World War II, concern with the small church shifted to its urban counterpart. Migrants from the rural south to the big cities of the north, black but also poor white, had been arriving since the early decades of the century. For many of these transplanted southerners, the bigness of established urban congregations was unsatisfactory. E. Franklin Frazier has described the move to recover the values of a small congregation:

The "storefront" church represents an attempt on the part of the migrants, especially from the rural areas of the South, to re-establish a type of church in the urban environment to which they were accustomed. They want a church, first of all, in which they are known as people. In the large city church they lose their identity completely and, as many of the migrants from the rural South have said, neither the church members nor the pastor know them personally. . . . In wanting to be treated as human beings, they want status in the church which was the main or only organization in the South in which they had status.[14]

These storefront churches also emerged as a model for a generation of white, middle-class Protestants who became the urban church missionaries of the 1940s and 1950s. Considered "young turks," these men and women contributed to a new style of small church in the heart of some of the nation's troubled cities. The East Harlem Protestant Parish, Oak Street Parish, and Chicago Westside Parish questioned the drive toward success and growth while they celebrated the possibility of ministry in the storefront.

For many other established urban congregations, however, the 1940s and 1950s meant hard times. The swift suburbanization of the nation in the quarter-century after World War II sapped the membership and financial resources of many grand old downtown congregations. Often without noticing the changes that had swept over them, these churches became small congregations with a haunting sense of being stranded and left behind. Pulpits which had once meant escape from the small town became symbols of failure and smallness as they were bypassed by the growing—big—suburban congregations. While in Boston we have seen such a church come to life again in its exciting mix of those people from the old congregation who hung on and the infusion of new life from recent migrants, we also know that many more such churches have simply grown smaller and smaller until the inevitable end.

Perhaps the best influence in the last twenty-five years on the problems and possibilities of the small congregation came through the renewal movement of the 1950s. In that period of unprecedented religious prosperity, a reaction set in against the large and presumably complacent suburban congregation. No more suburban captivity of the church! The. theological significance of what we know today as "small is beautiful" was translated by Gordon Cosby, of The Church of the Saviour in Washington, D.C., and others as "pure is better," that is, the pure Christian community would establish its distinctiveness over and against the world.

The renewalists developed a fresh, theologically informed understanding of the small congregation; yet that vision was not always transportable. A big difference remained between the experimental congregation that deliberately elects to be different and the settled congregation in a village in Maine or the business district of Chicago. To our dismay, we found that The Church of the Saviour could not be lifted out of Washington, D.C., and transposed elsewhere.

We don't expect to see the preoccupation with bigness and the admiration of the large church disappear overnight. Mass churches will characterize American Protestantism for some time to come. Across evangelical America, the dream of creating the largest and fastest-growing church is still very much alive and will remain so. This dream is evidenced in two books, *The Ten Largest Sunday Schools*, a best-seller written by Elmer Townes, and *America's Fastest Growing Churches*.

Our hope for the future is that other patterns will develop alongside the large church. In an industrial or agricultural society, the large church had many advantages and provided entertainment and diversion; but in a media society, the large church may be a handicap. ( By a *media society* we mean a society in the evolutionary stage in which the media are not only a system of communication but also a primary source of understanding ourselves as persons. )

Christian community is a fundamental problem in a media

society. Most of us are aware of the limitations of the nuclear family in providing unity or intimacy, and the extended family, except in certain enclaves, is a fading reality. Therefore, the need remains for an intermediate group, diverse, large, and encompassing enough to provide variety, yet small enough so that a sense of identity and support can develop.

Perhaps this hunger for closeness accounts in large part for the popularity of the human potential movement, for the cell and prayer groups of recent years, and for all the present searchings and fumblings for places where human beings can find closeness. Our guess is that the small congregation has a new possibility, a new occasion for understanding its life as an opportunity for human beings to know something of the joy of being a part of the oneness of the body of Christ.

One of us recently moved away from New York City. The element of life that will most be missed is the congregational support of a small church on the West Side of Manhattan. The city has provided all sorts of entertainment, but that congregation will be impossible to duplicate.

In any event, this brief historical survey raises some fundamental questions. Two are especially important. First, how do we develop a contemporary version of that eighteenth-century equity among ministers? How do we overcome those sharp distinctions between ministers serving small churches and those serving large congregations? We would suppose that question will lead to matters of equity and salary, but where else?

Second, how can we develop a serious theological critique of "boosterism" as an American value? Perhaps those who have received a sophisticated seminary education may feel such an exercise is unnecessary. While some persons may understand a theological critique of boosterism for growth and progress, of equating virtue with size, that criticism has not yet been understood by the vast reaches of American Protestantism. How does that message get across?

And most important, how can we recognize a new occasion, a fresh opportunity for the small congregation? How can the small congregation become a symbol and a sign of the future?

George Buttrick, the famous Presbyterian minister, once said, "In God's eye, there are no small churches." We have often wanted to ask Dr. Buttrick if, in God's eye, there are any large churches. His statement only reinforces, however ironically, the importance of size. How do we begin to deal with that?

The small congregation—white, black, rural, or urban—will probably survive as an American institution. The prophets of its demise, in 1887 or 1944, have not yet been sustained. The challenge for our generation can be in working for both strength and diversity in the churches—small and large—which will be found in the future.

## NOTES

1. Edward Bellamy, *Looking Backward* (New York: Ticknor and Co., 1887; reprint ed., New York: Random House, 1951) pp. 222–23.

2. Clarence Seidenspinner, "Church for Tomorrow," *The Christian Century* 61 (1944): 1132.

3. Harriet Beecher Stowe, *Oldtown Folks*, ed. Henry F. May (Cambridge: Harvard University Press, 1966), p. 88.

4. Harold Frederic, *The Damnation of Theron Ware*, ed. John Henry Raleigh (New York: Holt, Rinehart, and Winston, 1960) p. 12.

5. Agnes Sigh Turnbull, *The Bishop's Mantle* (New York: Macmillan, 1947).

6. Donald Scott, "From Office to Profession: A Social History of the New England Ministry, 1750–1850."

7. Lyman Beecher, *The Autobiography of Lyman Beecher*, ed. Charles Beecher, 2 vols. (New York: 1864; reprint ed., ed. Barbara M. Cross, Cambridge: Harvard University Press, 1961), 1:70.

8. Ibid.

9. Scott, "From Office to Profession."

10. Daniel J. Boorstin, *The Americans: The National Experience* (New York: Random House, 1965) p. 122.

11. Michael Lesy, *Wisconsin Death Trip* (New York: Pantheon Books, 1973).

12. Charles Josiah Galpin, *Empty Churches* (New York: Century, 1925) pp. 4–5.

13. Harvey Cox, *The Seduction of the Spirit* (New York: Simon & Schuster, 1973) p. 27.

14. E. Franklin Frazier, *The Negro Church in America* (New York: Schocken Books, 1964) p. 53.

# 2

# Social and Cultural Changes
# Affecting Small Congregations

---

## *Douglas W. Johnson*

I am troubled about small congregations. Partially, the uneasiness stems from experiences with small congregations throughout my pastoral career. As a student in southern Illinois I served very small congregations. Later the small congregation was a mission challenge in Chicago when I served as a pastor and member of a judicatory staff. Currently it is a major consideration in strategy development studies in which I work.

I am troubled because of the impossible institutional demands made on small congregations and the apparent unwillingness of church leaders to let them be and do what they can be and do best—develop human beings. An evaluation form returned by a pastor of a small congregation says it better than I:

> Your concerns are not our concerns. We are a small church interested in mission. Mission has been and will be a major emphasis for us. Your materials and procedures are not appropriate for us.

These words were his evaluation of an important and costly mission education program of a large denomination. He was not being unkind. He appreciated the stimulation of the material he regularly received, but the program was not helpful to the church he was serving.

His statement brings to light some dynamics of change which have produced a disjuncture between the institutional concerns of the denomination and the ministry of the small-membership church. Before turning to some of these dynamics which are external to the small church, I mention two internal factors, to emphasize that a church need not passively conform but can exercise some control over the form of its response.

## Internal Factors in the Response to Change

### Imminent Possibility

Change can be constructive or destructive. The primary requirement for creative change is identifying imminent possibilities. We isolate the possibilities according to our moods, and mood is critical for people and institutions. Recently, some news media have been accused of prolonging our general economic problem by creating and sustaining a mood of depression. Optimistic outlooks promote positive responses while expectations of failure produce disturbance and despair.

The mood of a congregation profoundly affects its responses to changes that affect its life. The changeover of lay leadership, the end of a pastor's regime, the movement into a community of a new ethnic group, and the change in location of an industry can all be turning points in the life of a church. How the congregation responds to these changes is affected in considerable measure by its mood or outlook. Recent case studies of churches in Indiana indicate that the mood of a church, when facing changing times, in large measure determines the church's size and potential. In addition, the members' feelings about themselves suggested the kind of life the congregations would have in the future.

## Control of Destiny

Small congregations exercise control over their destinies either by conscious deliberation or by sliding along in indecision. When they are indecisive, passivity curbs any creativity they possess. To be creative is to take the initiative, to find out who they are and what they can do. Usually it means compromising some dreams so that others may become realities. Human and institutional existence is based on compromises, on adapting to an environment.

*Workable compromises, however, can occur only when a person or institution has specific goals.* These are hard to articulate in small groups. Because of limited human resources, such groups find it easier to ascribe to unwritten goals or to those of a strong leader. There is a lack of continuity in this form of operation because, when a new leader comes along, new goals are established, sometimes without regard to the past.

While the mood and desire to control one's destiny are critical, they are internal to the group. No group lives in a vacuum. The external forces provide the arena in which internal life must be lived. Thus we must consider some important external factors small congregations have faced over the years.

## External Factors Affecting Small Churches

### Mobility

An outstanding trait of our society has been its high level of mobility. Since the early years of this century, this has focused on a movement from rural to urban locations. In 1890, for example,

65 percent of the U.S. population was rural. By 1920, the United States was an urban nation with 49 percent living in rural areas. This urban growth continued so that rural population had dropped to 27 percent in 1970.[1] In less than one hundred years we changed from a nonurban to an urban nation. Not only was this traumatic for the urban areas to which people moved and the rural communities they left, but it was also instrumental in reconstructing the American ethic.

A person cannot move from a personal to an impersonal society, which the rural to urban shift implies, without assuming new life-patterns. As we became an urban society, we developed nonparticipative means of recreation and substitute processes of communication. We had to adjust to complexity and to new forms of getting along with one another. The world was no longer limited by our rural values and institutions. We had to invent new social forms and processes.

This is not to put a plus or minus on the theater, movies, telephones, or other aspects of an urban world. I am pointing out the obvious. We could not change location by the millions and continue doing things in the same old ways.

The church felt the effects of this mobility in two ways. It saw the rise of large denominations, creatures of an urban myth that bureaucracies are effective means of program development in a shifting society. Second, the concentration of people made it important to attempt to coordinate, as well as develop, mission possibilities. Meanwhile, many small congregations, especially in nonmetropolitan areas, felt the wave of departures from the countryside, especially as their young adult children moved away in search of employment and established new lives, particularly in urban centers.

The pervasive aspect of mobility has been the urban mood it created in the society. Values became urbanized or, as societal analysts put it, impersonal and functional rather than personal and holistic. Even the remnant in the countryside now tends to hold essentially urban values when compared to earlier days of this century.

We must not forget that mobility affects churches in large urban centers also. As urban neighborhoods have grown old, they have experienced population flow-out. Mobility, which had brought young persons out of the countrysides and put them in the city, took them as older affluent adults to new places outside the city limits. People moved to suburbia, spurred on by rising affluence and the appeal of suburban developments. Racial changes have also been significant factors in the movement to suburbia, as have government housing subsidies through veteran's benefits and the Federal Housing Administration.

Church money and leadership follows the flow of people. Thus, in the 1940s and 1950s, church leaders concentrated on suburbia. There was a boom in church extension. *Comity* was the "in" word as denominations competed for the new pioneers. Churching became so competitive that, except in a few instances, there was a neglect of the needs of those churches in the cities and countryside which had supplied the parents and grandparents of suburban residents. For example, I worship in a beautiful building in a suburb with over one thousand members in the congregation. We have many programs. It is my children's church, but not really mine. Emotionally, I belong elsewhere. I feel more comfortable when I worship in my hometown, a 250-member congregation in the same building I remember as a boy. The forty-to-sixty-member churches at which I preached as a college student still abound in the surrounding communities.

A basic inequity in the church system affects the mood and possibilities of the small congregation. In a sense, my home church is paying a price for helping me become a minister. Many other small churches are also paying for developing their people. They pay a price because the people who are designing programs and developing ministries for our denominations are in churches like the one my children attend, not like the one in which I grew up.

I do not question the competency or dedication of persons in program development. The problem is their myopic life-view. They think all church institutions must function like our suburban congregation. I for one hope this is not the case. I do not need another half-trained psychology major "helping me get in touch with my family." I want personal relationships that count. I want substance and spirit, not jargon about human behavior.

Most of the people with whom I worship will leave the congregation in at least five years. I hesitate to attempt to relate in depth with them. Can we not find means to develop caring communities that exist in spite of mobility? I think so.

Mobility has made us fragmented and extroverted. It has stunted growth in the human encounters that matter and has separated us into different experience levels as it moved us into communities of similar economic and social tendencies.

In short, mobility has been responsible for large-scale population movements, a mood revolving around urban values, and separation of the church into quite different levels of experience and expectations. I fear, in the process, we have lost much of the sense of unity and diversity which is the church.

### Fluidity

Fluidity is another aspect of mobility. We flow into and out of each other's lives with scarcely a ripple. We have few common experiences to use in developing mutual concern or as a basis for encouraging interpersonal sharing. We go to a meeting. "Hi, I'm Bob—meet Joe." We talk a while and are gone. Who cares? Who shares?

Fluidity is most evident in our mode of transportation. A walking society is a talking society. A riding society is a listening society. A flying society is an impounded society. The speed with which we pass through and beyond our social or physical environment inhibits or encourages the development of meaningful human relationships.

At this point the strength of a small congregation can surface. Smallness provides the opportunity to develop lasting ties in an informal, caring setting. It must do this in face of strong societal forces. The urban values on which our church structures are based do not make it easy to realize this opportunity. The institutional climate forced onto small congregations may obliterate their opportunities to develop humanness. Value is often placed upon quickness, newness, and flashiness, attributes of an urban nation on the move. The small congregation must find ways to modify those values and stress human needs.

### "Ours" and Theirs"

Robert Frost said that one way to maintain friends is to build a fence between their properties—a good strong fence which allows the two parties easily to identify what belongs to the other.

This is a great philosophy when dealing with physical properties. In social settings, boundaries are hard to identify and difficult, if not impossible, to maintain. Yet each of us knows that social boundaries are real, and we can readily identify characteristics that separate us from other people. For example, a congregation may be, in the experience of a majority of its members, a supportive fellowship; however, the same congregation may practice subtle exclusion of newcomers because they are different. We live in a world of "ours" versus "theirs."

This social fact, to use Emile Durkheim's phrase, of "ours" and "theirs" may escape church people until they verbalize their feelings about newcomers versus old-timers, leaders versus followers, this family versus that family. When we say it this way, we begin to understand how social boundaries affect the church.

As a college student I served a small church. The members,

residents of an economically depressed area, were trying to find security in the church. I was assigned to the church, not called by the congregation. The members labeled me an "educated fool" before I had even preached. I was not one of them. The issues underlying this separation were conflicting life-styles, world views, theology, social milieu, security. The boundaries were real.

In the church we often try to hide or gloss over social boundaries; yet they are the stuff of which "ours" and "theirs" is made. Let me illustrate.

Think of a city. Los Angeles, Chicago, New York, Indianapolis, and London probably come quickly to mind. When my parents think of a city, Carlyle, Springfield, and St. Louis come first. The difference between the two lists lies in scale. In size and complexity these urban districts are worlds apart. Our images are entirely different even though the word *city* heads both lists. For all practical purposes, the place-names we call out separate us in world view, life-style, and expectation. We have different boundaries, limits, and standards.

When we are with a group of people who support our values, think our way, and share our history, they are "ours." When another group comes into our world, as new members in our congregation, as neighbors, as sons- or daughters-in-law, they are different. They are outlanders. We do not share an identity with them because we have not built bridges of common history, values, and world views. Even though we are together, we live in separate worlds.

Persons may belong to the same church even though their individual life-styles may be quite different. One group may use big words, dress in fancy clothes, and work in a neighboring city at professional jobs. Another group may be farmers who dress plainly, take trips now and then, and know the responsibility of owning their own businesses. When these two groups meet, they may act like oil and water. Psychologically they differentiate between "ours" and "theirs." They understand that their ideas, life expectations, and world views are not similar; yet it is possible for them to find agreement as they share similar values about youth, morals, or hopes for the future.

The mobility and fluidity of our society has produced a clash of "ours" and "theirs." New residents moving into established communities occasion clashes. These tensions become pronounced as the increase in nonurban population continues.

Calvin Beale, of the Economic Research Service of the U.S. Department of Agriculture, says:

> The vast rural-to-urban migration of people has been halted and, on balance, even reversed. During 1970–73 nonmetropolitan areas gained 4.2 percent in population compared to only 2.9 percent for metro areas.[2]

He also points out that the highest rates of nonmetropolitan growth are found among retirement counties, counties adjacent to metro areas, and counties with senior state colleges. What effect will this have?

Many Protestant congregations are found in such counties, in places of less than five thousand population. For example, 58.3 percent of United Methodist congregations are found in communities of fewer than one thousand persons, and 14.5 percent in populations of one thousand to five thousand. This means that 72.8 percent of the United Methodist churches are in communities of fewer than five thousand population.[3]

The potential for conflict increases when these established churches are faced with newcomers whose ages and values differ radically from those of the current residents.

The experience of congregations in dealing with such change is important. Data from Indiana suggest that when large numbers of new persons are incorporated rapidly the congregation actually changes membership. This does not mean that long-time members go off the books; they become less active. They may continue to give money because of their association with the church over the years, but they become inactive.[4]

Some congregations have endeavored to maintain a balance and develop programs according to needs. These small congregations thrive. In some places where there have not been serious attempts to build bridges between "ours" and "theirs," the result is an exclusive, stagnant, and dying congregation. This does not suggest that a real alternative for some congregations is not death. Death with integrity is and should continue to be an option. Death as a result of drift is not facing change creatively.

The way the congregation maintains its boundaries determines how it will deal with infusions of people, ideas, and morale.

### Institutions and People

Our final issue is related to the style difference between denominations and small congregations. People are individuals, but they are also social. They group themselves into social entities which provide the structures and organization for a continuing pursuit of common purposes. They entrust institutions with the maintenance of society.

An institution, no matter what its purposes, can be either a vehicle or an oppressor. As a vehicle, it can help people attain important goals in a socially acceptable way. For example, the institution of banking helps people with credit, savings, and the like. Judicial institutions maintain order and provide equal treatment through laws. But these same institutions can be oppressors. Anyone who has sought credit or dealt with a traffic officer giving a ticket knows what powerlessness means.

We like to think that the church is a vehicle through which we can find meaning and purpose in life. Seldom do we consider it an oppressor; yet congregations can become oppressors rather than vehicles of opportunity. Each of us can remember persons too embarrassed to come to worship because they did not have money to give; willing young people turned off by a dictatorial youth counselor; or a congregation sitting dutifully through the agonizing efforts of a choir. These are oppressive situations. The church allows the mediocre to predominate so often that a person may not find it in God's blessing and purpose.

This will need to change because the current social climate is emphasizing that institutions think in human terms and meet "people needs."

But what are these needs? One concern of people is that they grow and develop, at least enough to keep up with their peers. This means education, especially adult education. Every employed person receives some type of on-the-job training or personal counsel regarding new products, techniques, or means of working. They are growing and keeping up.

Another aspect of education is developing an avocation. A counselor recently reported his experience with an eighty-two-year-old woman who wanted help in planning to spend the next decade creatively. The result was that she enrolled in college for art training. Unusual? Not necessarily. Adult schools are important and, according to projections, will continue to gain acceptance. People also need moral and ethical education or training. The renewed interest in religious search is one indication of this need. Another is the increase in courses on religion in colleges and universities.

Another "people need" is to have some voice in decisions affecting oneself. This does not mean that people must have their way but that they need to feel they have been heard. Institutionally this is evident in police-community relations efforts and mail opinionaires from legislators.

Finally, people need to learn how to change. They feel pressures to change but often are unable to meet them. Group-training processes, psychological analyses, and simulation games are all designed to help people see the dynamics of change and react creatively.

One interesting finding in our Indiana study is that people in transitional churches cannot recognize change in the community. This is not surprising. They do not live in the community, and change has to be very obvious before they detect it. Change tends to be incremental and not dramatic.

The small congregation has been a leader in helping people meet their needs through intergenerational education, informal counseling, and sharing of leadership. One difficulty is that perhaps we have not learned from these situations and shared the lessons with others in similar circumstances. Instead of communicating our wisdom, we have focused on our inadequacies.

That is one reason this book holds promise for me, a troubled church person. It offers an opportunity to share our triumphs and defeats so that we can understand the humanity of the church. It is reminiscent of the woman who had interviewed members of another church as part of a research study. She said, "It made me feel real good to hear all their troubles. I am glad to know we aren't oddballs."

Skeptics may look on this effort as not being new, but they will be mistaken. We may try the same thing others have tried, but *we* are the new ingredients. Our enthusiasm for the search for new possibilities will certainly invigorate our lives and give others hope for a new era in the small congregation.

## NOTES

1. These and other data on population characteristics may be found in Helen Axel, ed., *A Guide to Consumer Markets, 1973, 1974* (New York: Conference Board, 1973); Conrad Taeuber and Irene B. Taeuber, *The Changing Population of the United States* (New York: John Wiley and Sons, 1958); and Fred K. Hines, David L. Brown, and John M. Zimmer, "Social and Economic Characteristics of the Population in Metro and Non-Metro Counties, 1970," Economic Research Service, U.S. Department of Agriculture, Agricultural Economic Report No. 272, Washington, D.C., 1975.

2. Calvin L. Beale, "The Revival of Population Growth in Non-metropolitan America," Economic Development Division, Economic Research Service, U.S. Department of Agriculture, June 1975, Washington, D.C.

3. These 1975 data on church membership by size of community for the United Methodist Church were supplied by Alan K. Waltz, United Methodist Church General Council on Ministries.

4. "Mission Strategy Development, A Task Force Report," North Indiana Conference, United Methodist Church, 1976.

# 3

# Types of Small Congregations and Their Implications for Planning

## *Douglas A. Walrath*

One of the most difficult tasks confronting church leaders and planners is to classify congregations into groups that will be useful for program planning and policy decision. Must every congregation be treated individually, or can they be combined into certain meaningful groups or types? On what basis or by what criteria should congregations be grouped for current and future policy making? When we discover programs or policies that are effective with a particular congregation, how do we know with which other congregations the same programs or policies are likely to be successful? When we observe certain patterns of change in the membership or the neighborhood surrounding a particular congregation, how do we know which other congregations are likely to experience similar changes? If we knew the answers to these questions, we could allocate available resources more effectively. We could help congregations discover programs that would be likely to succeed. We could help church leaders find and relate to other leaders in similar situations, and thus to share resources and strategies. While such insights are vital to all churches, they are particularly important for small congregations and those who work with them. Working with limited resources in changing or limiting social contexts, small congregations are often the least able to afford mistakes in program planning or policy decision.

The focus of this chapter is the classification of small congregations into types that will be useful for planning purposes and policy decision. We shall examine a three-dimensional classification system: (1) social context; (2) social position; and (3) church organization. The final section will deal with the interaction among types and the use of the classification system in church planning.

## Social Context Types

Classifying congregations according to social context assumes that what a congregation is and is likely to become is a product of the interaction between it and its environment. This approach seems valid because most persons experience the church as a part of the specific social context in which they live. They come to the church in that context, and the church forms a part of that context. This is important because most church planners and other professional church leaders tend to approach the church from an opposite point of view.

Church planning tends to be done largely by those who see the congregation as a local extension or outlet of a larger institution. Planners are nonlocal in their basic orientation and commitment. By contrast, most church participants are very local, both in orientation and commitment, and decisions made on the basis of denominational priorities or larger institutional commitments make little or no sense to them. Assumptions undergirding such decisions are contrary to the ethos that is basic to most church participants' experience. Examples of such assumptions are:

> It makes no sense to maintain two of our churches only six blocks apart.

> It is terribly inefficient for our denomination to maintain a church in the village and another only three miles away at the crossroads outside the village. Since the village church is the weakest of three mainline churches in the village, we could close it and let those attending it go to the other churches in the village or to the rural crossroads church.

Churches six blocks apart in a city may seem as though they are six miles apart to the participants if one church is in a middle-class, outer-urban neighborhood and the other is in a working-class neighborhood; they may seem sixty miles apart if the second is in an inner-city neighborhood.

Agricultural people living in a rural settlement, for whom the church is like an extended family, may find an impassable social gulf in a village church whose members are merchants and professionals. Few are able to cross back and forth in either direction. Likewise, a pastor attempting to serve a rural village church and a little crossroads church outside the village is likely to find that a style of preaching and ministry satisfactory to one group will not be so to the other.

Social context or social ecology is an important first dimension to consider in the process of classifying churches. People of similar or proximate social status tend to choose or are forced to locate in the same types of neighborhoods and communities. This is especially true in metropolitan regions. Likewise, persons who are demographically similar (same marital status, age group, and so forth) group together in regular patterns of residence and living. Hence, social groups are inclined to appear in regular patterns geographically.

Building upon previous work in the field of social or human

ecology and social stratification,[1] I have developed a series of metropolitan and nonmetropolitan social context types. A comprehensive, full description of these types is contained in two major reports published by the Synod of Albany, Reformed Church in America.[2] However, individual congregations can be classified simply by using brief descriptions of the types and by consulting a diagram. Such an overview appears here in Diagram 1.

Diagram 1 provides an ideal geographical distribution picture of the types. Actual classifying is occasionally complicated because a few areas will not fit obviously into a single type. Therefore, Tables 1–5, which appear at the end of this chapter, are included as a more extensive typology. One additional note: Because areas change, we may expect types to change; an area may begin as one type and become another. It is generally more useful for planning purposes to type an area on the basis of what it is becoming rather than on what it has been.

I have divided locales into two major regional groupings— metropolitan and nonmetropolitan. Metropolitan regions are basically those included in the Standard Metropolitan Statistical Area (SMSA) designation of the U.S. Census.[3] Nonmetropolitan regions are those outside the SMSA's. Exceptions occur because SMSA's by definition include complete counties, and occasionally locales within a county are simply too rural to be typed as functionally metropolitan.

Within the metropolitan region are three subgroups—cities, suburbs, and fringe zones which are subdivided into nine local areas. Moving from the center of the city out:

Type 1 is the Midtown locale, the city's central business district, usually the location for banks, large department stores, state or city office buildings.

Type 2 is an Inner City locale, generally one of the most deteriorating parts of the city with high incidence of social problems, rundown housing, and so on.

**Diagram 1**
**Social Context Typology: Geographical Pattern**

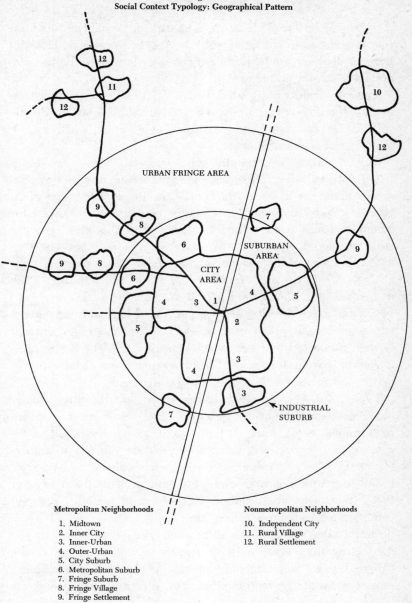

URBAN FRINGE AREA

SUBURBAN AREA

CITY AREA

INDUSTRIAL SUBURB

**Metropolitan Neighborhoods**

1. Midtown
2. Inner City
3. Inner-Urban
4. Outer-Urban
5. City Suburb
6. Metropolitan Suburb
7. Fringe Suburb
8. Fringe Village
9. Fringe Settlement

**Nonmetropolitan Neighborhoods**

10. Independent City
11. Rural Village
12. Rural Settlement

Type 3 is an Inner-Urban Neighborhood, basically residential but with some mixture of neighborhood-type businesses. Housing is generally two family, middle income, or lower-middle income, and its residents, ethnic groups.

Type 4 locales, designated Outer-Urban Neighborhoods, are toward the edges of the city. They have middle-class to upper-middle-class housing, almost entirely single family, and very few or no business establishments.

Moving out of the city to the suburbs, Type 5 locales are designated City Suburbs. These classic communities usually grew up along steam or electric transportation lines. They are aptly termed *sub-urb* because they emerged as places of residence for commuters who could afford to move out of the city. They are still considered prestige residential locations and have a community center and distinct community life.

Type 6 suburbs are designated Metropolitan Suburbs. They developed after the Second World War as residential neighborhoods encircling the city. They are arranged in a quiltlike pattern of residences, shopping centers, work areas, and entertainment centers connected by roads which ring the city. The basic transportation is around the ring rather than in and out of the city, via private automobile rather than public conveyance.

Type 7 suburbs, Fringe Suburbs, sprang up recently, usually along interstate highway systems. They relate to the entire metropolitan areas much the same as, in earlier times, City Suburbs related to the city. Fringe Suburbs are middle- to upper-middle-class residential areas for the newly affluent and younger middle-aged persons who are highly mobile. Zoning is strict, and there is little or no business. This grouping includes planned communities, sometimes called "new towns."

On the edge of the metropolitan area, where it expands into the nonmetropolitan area, we find two fringe types. Type 8, the Fringe Village, was originally an independent rural community, now overrun by the metropolitan area. Increasingly, housing has been purchased by younger middle-aged couples with children. These families seek a quiet village residence but one oriented toward the large metropolitan area. These communities tend toward combinations of long-term residents, middle-aged or older, and new arrivals.

On the edge of the fringe area are Fringe Settlements, or Type 9. These are former Rural Settlements; zoning is often poor, and land use unplanned and irregular. We find various types of housing, including mobile homes, older houses, newer suburban-type homes, and a few estates. There is still some agriculture, but most residents commute into the metropolitan area for employment.

In the nonmetropolitan region, we find first an urban area dominated by the Type 10 locale, Independent City. These cities have not given rise to a metropolitan region but stand alone, generally dependent on one major industry manufacturing one product for which raw materials are close at hand, for example, cement or bricks. As the industry has gone, so have the cities in recent times. Automation, synthetic substitutes, and foreign competition have all taken their toll. With reduced employment, many of these cities suffer urban blight. A fortunate few with an expanding industry (for example, higher education) have not declined.

The other area in the nonmetropolitan region is rural. It contains two local types, the first of which is Type 11, the Rural Village. This community is the traditional business, commercial, and social hub of a surrounding agricultural area. However, with the decline of agricultural workers over the last twenty years, many rural villages have either stayed the same size through out-migration of younger people or actually declined in population. The last nonmetropolitan type is Type 12, the Rural Settlement. It consists of a few houses, a small church, and sometimes one store or gas station, now closed because of the competition of neighboring villages and the lack of traffic due to the bypassing interstate highway system.

Each locale has a characteristic church. What that church will generally be like is determined by the locale and the types of persons available to it. Specifically, the churches may be described as follows.

The Type 1, or Midtown, congregation is usually large in size, occupies a large building, has multiple staff and middle- to upper-middle-class membership with excellent programs and resources.

Type 2 in the Inner City is usually a struggling, heavily subsidized parish or a new development such as a storefront, seeking to minister to the new social groups in the area. These are generally lower socioeconomic groups, with characteristics different from those for whom the original building was built if, indeed, the original building is still utilized.

Type 3 in the Inner-Urban Neighborhood is usually a church that has lost a significant number of members in the last twenty-five years due to death, neighborhood change, and mobility. Many of its members have moved to the suburbs or to other areas in connection with retirement or business transfers. Those still active are middle-aged to older persons who live in the neighborhood or who grew up in it, moved to the suburbs, and now drive back to support the church. Often the church has little interaction with those who are new to the neighborhood. Newcomers are of a different social or ethnic group with whom the original members find interaction difficult. Very small Type 3 churches are usually composed of those few old members who still live in the neighborhood.

The Type 4 church in the Outer-Urban Neighborhood traditionally has been family centered. Recently, however, a drop in the number of younger children in the population that has traditionally been active has led to severe church school decline. The church now faces an older, middle-aged membership with teenage children, if children are still present. Many of its members have moved to the suburbs. Its proximity to the suburbs makes their return more likely on Sunday mornings than is the case in Type 3, but it begins to see a future similar to the experience of its Inner-Urban counterpart, and in time if the area becomes Type 3, so will the church.

The City Suburb church in the Type 5 locale resembles the Type 1 church in Midtown. It is generally large in size, affluent, often with staff ministry, and a quality program, but a participating congregation much like the one described in the Outer-Urban Neighborhood area. If its area becomes a functional part of the city, the church may change to an Urban Neighborhood church.

Type 6, or Metropolitan Suburban, congregations usually have a nuclear-family-centered program and a large church school. This reflects their orientation to the younger middle-aged residents that inhabited Metropolitan Suburbs in the postwar years when these congregations experienced their most rapid growth. Now they are composed of more persons in their forties and early fifties, indicating the loss of appeal of Metropolitan Suburbs to younger adults. Thus, Type 6 suburbs are beginning to feel like Type 5 suburbs, though a few have young adult apartment dwellers available to them.

Type 7 congregations are products of recent rapid suburban growth. Some are new-church development projects. They have more families with younger children than any of the types seen so far. Many continue to grow, both in membership and in church school attendance, particularly when they have a population of nuclear families favorably inclined toward a conservative, traditional, family-centered church.

Fringe Village churches, or Type 8, experienced some growth in the late sixties to early seventies. This pattern has moderated with the decrease in geographical mobility and with the declining interest in organized religion on the part of middle-class persons. These churches have often been scenes of conflict between new arrivals and traditional village residents. Now, the new arrivals have by and large withdrawn from activity, leaving the church to the traditional residents, now considerably reduced in number and advanced in age. With their small size and loss of appeal to new persons in the available population, many Fringe Village churches face a bleak future.

Type 9, or the Fringe Settlement church, most often remains small because it is unable to attract many new members in spite of the fact that the area around it has grown. Its limited size and characteristic ingrown attitude limit programming ability and make it a tightknit, familial group not easy for the newcomer to enter.

In the nonmetropolitan region, the urban churches in the Independent Cities, Type 10, have declined seriously throughout the late sixties and early seventies as population of the Independent Cities has itself declined and grown older. The social groups who supported many of these congregations are now composed of ethnic groups different from those to whom the churches generally appealed.

Rural Village churches, Type 11, have experienced decline in the last ten years due to the loss of population from the rural areas. The remaining participants are middle-aged to older persons. Few young adults are available to these congregations because there are simply few of them in the area.

Most Rural Settlement churches, Type 12, the smallest of the rural churches, have remained stable in size over the last ten years. This is probably due to nonfarm rural residents replacing those who move out of the area with the decline in agricultural employment. Newcomers are persons who want to live in an uncongested area and who affirm the rural value system, which includes the small church.

## Social Position Types

A second method of classifying churches is by social position, which may be defined as the church's "posture" or position of influence in relation to the community or neighborhood. We may designate three postures: A. Dominant; B. Subordinate; C. Exclusive.

The church in a Dominant, or Type A, social position is the prestige church. It is usually larger than churches around it. Old families, old money, and powerful people tend to be members. Examples are "Old First," the large prestige church in midtown; the "Church on the Green," with the tallest spire in the center of a City Suburb; "Old First" in the Independent City center; *the* church in a Rural Village. The Dominant church is seen as the leader, the outstanding one, the winner.

The Subordinate, or social position Type B, church is the "other church" in a village, the one in the middle of the block in Midtown. It is "Second Church," the one outside the village. In any yoke or cluster, it is the dependent church, clearly in some other church's shadow.

The third social position is Type C, Exclusive. It relates to a specific group and is seen as relating to the needs and interests of that group. Examples are a Roman Catholic national parish that relates to an ethnic group, the ethnic Protestant church (for example, a church of Dutch immigrants), a small congregation in a rural area that is dominated by one extended family or a very small group of families, a house church, a theologically conservative congregation with rigid theological and social requirements for membership, and so on. The Exclusive congregation is in a real sense noncompetitive with the other two social position types. Its exclusiveness may be overt and intentional or implied and not obvious to the members. Its entrance requirements make its formal or informal exclusiveness apparent to outsiders. For example, the theologically conservative congregation requires a certain set of beliefs and certain moral behavior of those who wish to become members. In the family congregation the social relationships may be so closely knit that the outsider has great difficulty breaking in. The small neighborhood congregation composed of members who formerly lived in the neighborhood may express desires to interact with the new neighborhood residents who are of a different social and ethnic group, but its exclusiveness makes such interaction highly unlikely.

Certain interactions between social context and social position types are immediately apparent. For example, a Dominant church in a Rural Village is likely to have a very different history and future than a Subordinate church in the same context. If the village is declining as a business and professional center and if new arrivals are middle to lower-middle class, the traditionally Dominant church will find its future less promising than the Subordinate church. Likewise, it will be more difficult to persuade the members of a Dominant church to participate in any kind of adjustment such as a cluster or a team ministry. On the other hand, the Subordinate church in the same village may find such adjustment palatable. It is important in planning and in policy considerations to note, not only the social context in which the church functions, but the position that it occupies within that context.

## Church Organization Types

*Independent.* The Independent church programmatically and in terms of leadership stands by itself. It has its own pastor and perhaps its own staff. It sees itself as producing all the program and church life which its members require or desire. Any outside help is viewed as occasional and temporary. Indeed, if it needs help of any kind of an ongoing basis, church members experience a sense of failure, that the church is not what it should be.

*Yoke.* The Yoke (one minister serves two or more congregations) is probably the weakest and also the most popular interchurch link. Congregations usually enter it out of a sense of weakness. Single congregations lacking the resources to pay a pastor pool their economic resources in order to employ a minister. The weakness of the Yoke is that it involves no planned cooperation or social interaction between the churches involved. Each places its demands upon the common minister independently, often without any cognizance of the demands being placed upon him or her by the other(s). Only the minister can resolve the tension, and often he or she does so by absorbing it. Generally speaking ministers who serve in yoked parishes are dissatisfied with the arrangement.

*Team Ministry.* Team Ministry may be defined as two or more pastors cooperating to serve one or more congregations. In a Team Ministry, there is no formal structure involving representatives of the several congregations. There is, however, some agreement, either formal or informal, among all the congregations to accept the services of more than one pastor. Pastors generally are more satisfied with a Team Ministry than with a yoked parish for two reasons. First, they experience the mutual support of a team. Other team members provide sympathetic understanding and other forms of human-spiritual encouragement. Second, given the larger population base of several combined congregations, each minister is able to utilize his or her special skills more extensively. If, for example, a team member has counseling expertise, through referral by other team members he or she is able to exercise it among more persons. The team member with skills in youth work may undertake it with young people from several congregations.

*Cluster.* In the Cluster two or more congregations cooperate programmatically. This involves formal organization which brings together representatives of the cooperating congregations for planning and program execution on a *regular* basis. A Cluster may look like a Yoke when only one minister serves the several congregations. The difference is that the Cluster involves interface among representatives of the congregations on an ongoing basis and not just interaction through the pastor. Clusters may include only one dimension of the life of the congregation as, for

example, a program cluster for the purposes of youth work; or
they may embrace a nearly total interaction in the lives of the
congregations. Clusters are generally more satisfying, both to the
minister and to the congregations, because of the greater openness and accountability.

*Cluster-Team.* This type is simply a combination of Team
Ministry and Cluster. It involves two or more ministers serving
two or more congregations. There is ongoing planned cooperation
among the ministers and a structure in which representatives of
the congregations participate. Cluster-Team may encompass only
one or nearly all dimensions of the lives of the congregations.
Cluster-Team is, generally speaking, the strongest form of interchurch cooperation. For that reason, it has the most potential for
program development. It also poses the greatest threat to individual congregations. The Cluster-Team can become so effective
that it overshadows individual congregations. The opportunities
of the Cluster-Team can become so satisfying and challenging to
the ministers that they neglect their responsibility to the individual congregational units. Thus, while the Cluster-Team has the
most potential, it also requires the most organizational maintenance.

## Application

Diagram 2 is a three-dimensional picture of the classification
system we have been discussing and illustrates social context,
social position, and church organization. Each type has its peculiar characteristics, patterns of change, and potentials. Close
attention to these will allow church leaders to forecast developments in churches of various types and to build upon natural
inclinations of the several types, saving a great deal of frustration
and at times even heading off disaster. The classification system
will be especially helpful to those who work with small congrega-

**Diagram 2**
**Type Matrix of Local Churches**

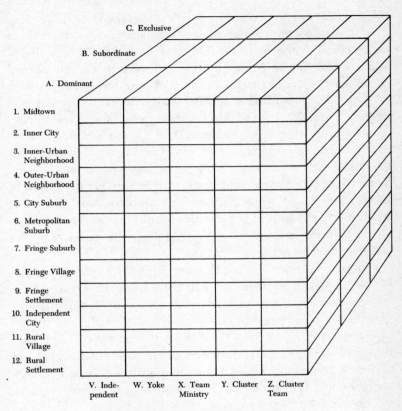

1–12 indicate social context (neighborhood); A–C indicate
social position; V–Z indicate type of church organization.

tions. The peculiar vulnerability of small congregations makes a solid base for policy decision essential. Poor policy decisions which lead to further weakening of an already weak and small congregation may be sufficient to push it over the brink.

Of the three dimensions of the classification system, church organization is the most feasible as a basis for change efforts. While social context is least open to influence by church leaders, social position is not much more so. For example, a congregation in a socially Subordinate position could develop program and employ professional leadership to attract persons who would help it move into a Dominant position. But the move would not be easy to make since persons who would be attracted to a socially Dominant congregation are likely to be involved in one already. Thus, planning efforts should begin with identifying the givens of social context and social position and move on to determining which form(s) of social organization would be possible, building on the natural inclinations of the congregation. Some examples will help to clarify this process.

A Rural Village church (Context Type 11) that is socially Dominant (Position Type A) will most likely be open only to Independent organization (Organization Type 1). Such a congregation is accustomed to viewing itself as self-sufficient. It pays its own way; it does its own thing. Even if it falls upon hard times through loss of members, it may do better with a "tentmaker," or part-time minister. Because he or she ministers only to that congregation and thus is identified as *the* pastor of the congregation, a Dominant congregation prefers this type of pastor to sharing a pastor. On the other hand, a Rural Village church that is socially Subordinate (Position Type B) will generally be open to other options such as yoking, teaming, or clustering. This type of church will cooperate simply because it has less to lose in terms of self-image. It will be open to organizational cooperation with Rural Settlement, as well as with other Subordinate congregations.

Rural or Fringe Settlement churches (Context Types 9 or 12) typically are socially Subordinate (Position Type B), and, therefore, open to various coordinated efforts with one another and with village churches which are also Subordinate. However, small Settlement churches that are socially Exclusive (Position Type C), for example, those that are theologically conservative or dominated by one extended family, will not usually be open to coordinated efforts or will participate in them reluctantly. In any event, protecting the independence of the Exclusive church in joint organizational efforts will be important to its continued participation.

A small Inner-Urban Neighborhood congregation (Context Type 3) that is Exclusive (Position Type C), because it is composed of the few remaining members of a social group that has largely moved out of the neighborhood, will find it very difficult to cooperate programmatically with churches reaching the current residents. This is especially true if the congregation was at one time in a socially Dominant position. The most effective policy decision may simply be to support the congregation with part-time leadership until there are not enough old members left to continue and then begin a new work either through modifying the old building or by abandoning it. The new work can be carried on with indigenous groups that are either socially Dominant or socially Subordinate.

A new church development which takes the form of a "house church" in a Fringe Suburb (Context Type 7), because of rigid discipline and lack of visibility (no church building), will probably include only a small number of members. These will be the few area persons to whom rigid discipline appeals. The congregation may never expand to become a Dominant institution including large segments of the neighborhood because people see it as exclusive and identify with it only if its style appeals to them.

We could continue to duplicate examples, but church leaders

## TABLE 1
### Social Context Typology, City Area
### (in Metropolitan Region 50,000+ population)

*Note*: In larger metropolitan centers, urban types (1–4) may appear in *politically* separate civil jurisdictions. These are technically suburbs, but ecologically they are integrated with a dominant city. Probably they are best visualized as *sub-cities*, smaller urban centers containing neighborhoods of Types 1–4. Suburbs may be related ecologically as much or more to these smaller urban centers as they are to the dominant central city.

| Neighborhood Type, Characteristics, and Change Pattern (1960–70) | Net Tract Density (1970) | Church Membership Location and Change Pattern (1965–75) |
| --- | --- | --- |
| **Type 1: Midtown** Traditional center of city. Area is often only slightly deteriorated. Light and "unobjectionable" businesses, professional and commercial offices and institutions. Area is viewed as a relatively safe neighborhood, though close proximity of a Type 2 (Inner City) neighborhood may affect the safety and image of the Type 1 area. Area is seen as relatively accessible and is often one of the areas most frequented by suburban residents. Population change: Moderate decrease, −10 to −25%. | High. Averages 6,000 to 12,000 persons per sq. mi. | The majority of members live some distance away, either in various neighborhoods of the city or in suburbs. They are drawn to the church probably because of size, quality and purposefulness of program, quality of leadership, image of church, etc. These churches are traditional, higher status, large-size "First Churches." Membership change pattern: Stable to slow attrition, 0 to −9%. |

**TABLE 1** (*continued*)

| Neighborhood Type, Characteristics, and Change Pattern (1960–70) | Density (1970) Net Tract | Church Membership Location and Change Pattern (1965–75) |
| --- | --- | --- |
| **Type 2: Inner City** Multiunit dwellings. Neighborhood deteriorated. Very poor housing. High incidence of social problems. Mixed commercial and residential. Usually ethnic succession has occurred, sometimes more than once. Lower socio-economic groups predominate. Population change: Moderate to rapid decrease, −10 to −50%. Severe population loss seems related to neighborhood deterioration and/or highway construction. | Very high to extremely high. Averages 12,000 to 15,000+ persons per sq. mi. | Majority of members live in neighborhood around church. Church is "indigenous"; a majority of the leadership is drawn from groups now living in the neighborhood. Membership change pattern: Inconsistent. |
| **Type 3: Inner-Urban Neighborhood** Mixed business and residential, middle and lower income, two-family housing or apartments. May be more commercial than residential. May be industry close by. Young adults and older persons predominate. Generally more Roman Catholics | High to very high. Averages 6,000 to 15,000 persons per sq. mi. | Members are residents of neighborhood and long-standing members living in other neighborhoods or in suburban residential areas. Proportion of members living in immediate neighborhood seems related to amount of business, commerce, and industry |

TABLE 1 (*continued*)

| Neighborhood Type, Characteristics, and Change Pattern (1960–70) | Net Tract Density (1970) | Church Membership Location and Change Pattern (1965–75) |
|---|---|---|
| than Protestants. Close to center of city or in an older industrial suburb. Population change: Moderate decrease, −10 to −25%. | | in area around church. Where business and commerce predominate, more participants may live some distances from church. Where area is residential for new ethnic groups and/or industry is close by, more participants may live near church. Membership change pattern: Rapid attrition, −26 to −50%. Rate tends to decrease as life-cycle advances. |
| **Type 4: Outer-Urban Neighborhood** Predominantly residential middle income, single or two-family houses. Some small businesses. Usually ethnic changes occurring. Proportion of Roman Catholic and/or Jewish population usually increasing. Protestants usually decreasing. Younger adults and older persons well represented. With increased population of ethnic groups, Type 4 may become | High-moderate to high. Averages 2,500 to 12,000 persons per sq. mi. | Members live in the neighborhood near the church and in other neighborhoods both in the city and residential suburbs, the last group including many of long-standing membership. Size of suburban group seems associated with church size and distance church is located from urban core. Generally, the farther the church is or the more protected it is from the center |

TABLE 1 (*continued*)

| Neighborhood Type, Characteristics, and Change Pattern (1960–70) | Net Tract Density (1970) | Church Membership Location and Change Pattern (1965–75) |
|---|---|---|
| Type 3. Some Type 4 areas on edges of city resemble suburban areas, may even be contiguous with a suburban neighborhood. Population change: Stable to slight increase, 0 to 3%. | | city, the larger it is and the larger the proportion of suburban participants. Membership change pattern: Moderate attrition, −10 to −25%. Tendency for rate to increase as life-cycle advances. |

## TABLE 2
### Social Context Typology, Suburban Area
### (in Metropolitan Region 50,000+ population)

| Community Type and Change Pattern (1960–70) | Net Tract Density (1970) | Services Available, Activity, and Development Pattern | Churches' Change Pattern (1965–75) |
|---|---|---|---|
| **Type 5:** **City Suburb** Older suburban areas; period of rapid growth began usually by 1940. Traditionally viewed as prestige residential locations. Usually | Varies considerably within area with cost of housing and proximity to central city. Generally low-moderate to moderate. Averages 700 | All utilities generally available. Usually a community business district, now challenged by shopping centers. Strict zoning. Little | Moderate attrition, −10 to −25%. |

TABLE 2 (*continued*)

| Community Type and Change Pattern (1960–70) | Net Tract Density (1970) | Services Available, Activity, and Development Pattern | Churches' Change Pattern (1965–75) |
|---|---|---|---|
| closer to and developed more in relation to central cities than Type 6. Population change: Moderate increase, 10 to 25%. | to 2,500 persons per sq. mi. | industry. Moderate- to high-cost single-family housing. Areas developed after 1945 may consist of units built simultaneously, but each house will tend to be individually "styled," and per unit value will tend to be higher than per unit value in recently developed areas of Type 6. | |
| **Type 6: Metropolitan Suburb** New or middle-aged suburban residential area; period of rapid growth began usually in the | Varies considerably with stage of area development and cost of housing. Generally low to | Public sewage disposal and water supply available. Shopping centers. Usually some "un- | Moderate growth turning to slight loss, 25 to −9% |

TABLE 2 (*continued*)

| Community Type and Change Pattern (1960–70) | Net Tract Density (1970) | Services Available, Activity, and Development Pattern | Churches' Change Pattern (1965–75) |
|---|---|---|---|
| 1950s or 60s. Development stage related to improvements in highway systems and to other developments within metropolitan area. Population change: Rapid increase, 26 to 50%. | moderate. Averages 200 to 2,500 persons per sq. mi. | objectionable" industry. Single-family, moderate-cost housing. Sizable amount of residential building projected and/or in process. Some "mass-produced" housing, with whole residential areas with many identical or near identical units built at the same time. Quiltlike land use pattern of interrelated areas of residence, work, shopping, recreation, etc. Recent construction includes apartment houses, condominiums. | |

TABLE 2 (*continued*)

| Community Type and Change Pattern (1960–70) | Net Tract Density (1970) | Services Available, Activity, and Development Pattern | Churches' Change Pattern (1965–75) |
|---|---|---|---|
| **Type 7: Fringe Suburb** Newly developed suburban area (or "New Town") in urban fringe zone adjacent to highly developed metropolitan core. Growth pattern clearly related to interstate highway systems which make metropolitan core easily accessible. Population change: Extremely rapid increase, over 50%. | Varies with stage of development and cost of housing. Generally low. Averages 200 to 700 persons per sq. mi. | Public sewage disposal and water supply available or projected. "Planned" communities and/or strict zoning. Density tightly controlled. Moderate- to higher-cost single-family housing in homogeneous neighborhoods. "Club" type social organization. Area viewed as new high status residential location. Little or no industry. Only controlled shopping areas permitted. | Rapid growth, over 50%. New church development pattern of rapid growth followed by stability. |

# TABLE 3
## Social Context Typology, Urban Fringe Area
### (in Metropolitan Region 50,000+ population)

| Community Type and Change Pattern (1960–70) | Area (Township) Density (1970) | Services Available, Activity, and Development Pattern | Churches' Change Pattern (1965–75) |
|---|---|---|---|
| **Type 8: Fringe Village** A former Rural Village; historically, relatively independent; now strongly related to a metropolitan region. Population change: Moderate increase, 10 to 25%. | Low. Averages 200 to 700 persons per sq. mi. | Usually public sewage disposal and water supply. Some business center. Little or no industry. Moderate population increase, usually controlled by careful zoning. Moderate-cost housing predominates (some two-family). Increase of new, middle-class, well-educated persons. | Slow to moderate attrition, −3 to −25%. |
| **Type 9: Fringe Settlement** Settlement or very small village, formerly a Rural Settlement; historically, relatively independent; now strongly dominated by a metropolitan region. Population change: | Very low. Averages 100 to 200 persons per sq. mi. | Usually no public sewage disposal or water supply. Little or no business center. Accelerating population growth. Moderate to low-cost housing predominates. Scat- | Stable or very slight loss, 0 to −3%. |

TABLE 3 (*continued*)

| Community Type and Change Pattern (1960–70) | Area (Township) Density (1970) | Services Available, Activity, and Development Pattern | Churches' Change Pattern (1965–75) |
|---|---|---|---|
| Rapid increase, 26 to 50%. | | tered upper-middle-class housing. Mixed land usage and housing; inconsistent zoning. | |

## TABLE 4
### Social Context Typology, Urban Area
### (Nonmetropolitan Region)

| Community Type, Size, and Change Pattern (1960–70) | City Density (1970) | Services Available and Activity Pattern | Churches' Change Pattern (1965–75) |
|---|---|---|---|
| **Type 10:**<br>**Independent City**<br>A small city, not surrounded by vast suburban developments, which has not given rise to a metropolitan region (SMSA). Population range: 2,500 to 49,999. Population change: Slow decrease, −4 to −9%. | High moderate. Averages 2,500 to 6,000 persons per sq. mi. | Public sewage disposal and water supply. Business center. One or more industries of some size; employment center. Some urban phenomena, especially in larger areas. May be some long-range commuting to a metropolitan area for employment. | Moderate attrition, −10 to −25%. |

**TABLE 5**
**Social Context Typology, Rural Area**
**(Nonmetropolitan Region)**

| Community Type, Size, and Change Pattern (1960–70) | Area (Township) Density (1970) | Services Available and Activity Pattern | Churches' Change Pattern (1965–75) |
|---|---|---|---|
| **Type 11: Rural Village**<br>Village, 250 to 2,499 population. Population change: Stable to slight decrease, 0 to −3%. | Very low. Averages 100 to 200 persons per sq. mi. | Some public sewage disposal and/or water supply. Some industry may be present. Village serves as a business and service center for surrounding area. May be some long-range commuting to a metropolitan area for employment. | Stable to slow attrition, 0 to −9% |
| **Type 12: Rural Settlement**<br>Open country or settlement of less than 250 persons. Population change: Moderate increase, 10 to 25%. | Extremely low. Averages under 100 persons per sq. mi. | No public sewage disposal or water supply. Little or no business or industry. May be some long-range commuting to a metropolitan area for employment. | Stable to slow attrition, 0 to −9% |

will be able to develop catalogs of their own by working with the typology. Those who employ the classification system will discover that they accumulate a reservoir of systematic information which permits more intelligent and helpful policy decisions, leading to maximum growth for congregations for which they are responsible as well as better stewardship of the church's resources.

## NOTES

1. These include: James West, *Plainville, U.S.A.* (New York: Columbia University Press, 1945); W. Lloyd Warner, Marsha Meeker, and Kenneth Eells, *Social Class in America* (Chicago: Science Research Associates, 1949); August B. Hollingshead, *Elmtown's Youth* (New York: John Wiley & Sons, 1949); August B. Hollingshead, "The Two-Factor Index of Social Position," mimeographed (1957); John F. Cuber and William F. Kenkel, *Social Stratification in the United States* (New York: Appleton-Century-Crofts, 1954); Arthur J. Vidich and Joseph Bensman, *Small Town in Mass Society* (Garden City, N.Y.: Doubleday, 1960); Bernard Barber, *Social Stratification* (New York: Harcourt, Brace and World, 1957); N. J. Demerath, III, *Social Class in American Protestantism* (Chicago: Rand McNally, 1965); Manfield Stanley, "Church Adaptation to Urban Social Change: A Typology of Protestant City Congregations," *Journal for the Scientific Study of Religion,* 2 (1962): 64–73; Gerhard Lenski, *The Religious Factor* (Garden City, N.Y.: Doubleday, 1961); R. D. McKenzie, "Ecology, Human," *Encyclopedia of the Social Sciences,* vol. 5 (New York: Macmillan, 1931); R. D. McKenzie, *The Metropolitan Community* (New York and London: McGraw-Hill, 1933); Alvin Boskoff, *The Sociology of Urban Regions* (New York: Appleton-Century-Crofts, 1962); Robert E. Park, ed., *The City* (Chicago: University of Chicago Press, 1925), Samuel W. Blizzard and William F. Andersen, "Problems in Rural-Urban Fringe Research: Conceptualization and Delineation," *Progress Report 89* (State College, Pa.: Pennsylvania State College Agricultural Experiment Station, 1952); Noel P. Gist, "Ecological Decentralization and Rural-Urban Relationship," *Rural Sociology* 17 (1952):328–335; Miles W. Rodehaver, "Fringe Settlement as

a Two-Directional Movement," *Rural Sociology* 12(1947):49–57; Stuart A. Queen and David B. Carpenter, "The Sociological Significance of the Rural-Urban Fringe from the Urban Point of View," *Rural Sociology* 18(1953):102–8; Homer Hoyt, *The Structure and Growth of Residential Neighborhoods in American Cities* (Washington, D.C.: Federal Housing Administration, 1939); Homer Hoyt, "Recent Distortions of Classical Models of Urban Structure," *Land Economics* 40(1964):199–212; Eric Goode, "Social Class and Church Participation," *The American Journal of Sociology* 72(1966):102–11; Liston Pope, "Religion and the Class Structure," *The Annals of the American Academy of Political and Social Science* 256 (1948):84–91; Louis Bultena, "Church Membership and Church Attendance in Madison, Wisconsin," *American Sociological Review* 14(1949):384–89; Joseph Kahl, *The American Class Structure* (New York: Holt, Rinehart, and Winston, 1957); Joseph Kahl and James Davis, "A Comparison of Indexes of Socio-Economic Status," *American Sociological Review* 20(1955):317–25.

2. Douglas Walrath, "The Congregations of the Synod of Albany, Reformed Church in America," Parts I and II, mimeographed (Schenectady: Synod of Albany, 1970); and "The Congregations of the Synod of Albany, Reformed Church of America," Part V, mimeographed (Schenectady: Synod of Albany 1974).

3. The U.S. Census defines an SMSA: "except in the New England States, a standard metropolitan statistical area is a county or group of contiguous counties which contains at least one city of 50,000 inhabitants or more, or 'twin cities' with a combined population of at least 50,000. In addition to the county or counties containing such a city or cities, contiguous counties are included in an SMSA if, according to certain criteria, they are socially and economically integrated with the central city. In the New England States, SMSA's consist of towns and cities instead of counties."

# 4

# The Real and the Unreal: Social and Theological Images of the Small Church

## *Arthur C. Tennies*

My concern here is to describe and analyze the theological and social images of small churches that are primary in our denominations, particularly among the leadership, and to compare them to reality. Many of these images are inaccurate and negative and should be replaced by positive ideas of what small churches can be and accomplish.

## The Importance of Images

Images are important because they have the power to motivate or immobilize. If people, individually or collectively, have positive images of themselves that provide a sense of worth and a conviction that they are capable, they will be motivated to live out the images. If people have negative self-images and see themselves as worthless and incapable, they are likely to be immobilized. For example, a number of studies have shown how images govern children's ability to learn. A teacher who believes that a low-achieving student can be a high achiever will communicate that conviction, and the child may move toward a new image.[1]

Images provide patterns for the future. People attempt to shape events so that the future will conform to the patterns. Without positive images, people have no guide for their efforts to make things better in the future than they are in the present.

Images provide frameworks for the interpretation of events and information. A negative image of a small church will magnify the church's faults and weaknesses and will minimize or obscure its strength and accomplishments. Of course, the reverse is also true.

Any discussion must deal with generalizations and typical cases, but there is no typical small church. I have chosen to limit the kinds I will consider. It would be presumptuous for me to attempt to deal with ethnic and racial small churches. Most of my experience has been with rural small churches, and mainly I will have those in mind. This is a sound approach since a large percentage of the predominantly white small churches are rural, and many church leaders have had their images shaped by experiences with such churches.

While I want to correct unnecessary images and stress the importance and possibilities of small churches, I am aware of the danger in doing so. Often, movements in the church become so enthusiastic that they end up replacing false negative images with false positive ones. It is important to guard against that tendency and to be as realistic as possible. Small churches face real problems of size, and these are at the root of some negative images. Most of these problems—lack of adequate resources, inadequate facilities and equipment, short pastorates, and so on— are dealt with elsewhere in this book and need not be repeated here. Nevertheless, we must acknowledge these problems as real. On the other hand, some negative images of small churches are based on assumptions and unrealistic expectations that should be challenged.

### The Role of Social Factors in the Development of Images

Various social factors shape the images we hold of small churches. How do these factors help create negative images of small churches and positive images of large ones? Compare a one-hundred-fifty-member church and a nine-hundred-member church. Both situations are hypothetical, but the differences between them frequently occur in real life and have played an important role in creating popular images.

One is simply size or what may be called the critical mass factor. The pastor of the small church calls a meeting to talk about hunger or to study the prophets, and four people show up. They think of all the people not there, become discouraged, and drop the effort. The pastor of the large church calls a similar meeting, and twenty-four people come. They soon have an interested group of enthusiastic people. At a clergy association meeting, the large-church pastor describes the concern members have shown for the programs, and the small-church pastor wishes he or she had such members. The fact is, members of the large church are proportionately no more interested than those in the small church. In both cases, 2.7 percent of the membership responded, but in one situation, that small percentage produced a critical mass—twenty-four people—and in the other it did not. Whatever the program issue, the pastor of the large church can soon have a group of enthusiastic lay people helping to promote that concern within the congregation; in the small church the pastor tends to remain a lonely voice.

Consider a typical Sunday morning. The small-church pastor

preaches to the faithful few. He or she is lucky to speak to sixty people. The large-church pastor preaches to a comfortably filled sanctuary, with at least two hundred fifty people. Which pastor is actually preaching to the faithful few? Attendance in the small church is 40 percent of membership, and in the large church, 28 percent.

The difference in size is a factor in a variety of other circumstances. The small church may have twelve senior-high young people, while the large church has eighty. The youth group of the small church struggles along with six participants while that of the large church sails ahead with twenty-four. But it is the small church that is doing the better job of involving its youth; 50 percent participate as compared with 30 percent in the large church. In program after program the large church, by involving a select few, appears more vital, but the small church is doing the better job of involving its members. What counts is the critical mass and the appearance of success that this brings.

Size is also important in regard to lay leadership. The ratio of leadership to members is typically much higher in the large church, making it possible to pick and choose; in the small church, a much larger percentage of the membership must assume leadership whether qualified or not.

Size has often been an important, but unexpressed, assumption in the resource materials made available to churches. For instance, the closely graded Sunday school with a class for each age group was for a number of years considered the ideal. If a church was to have a good Sunday school, it had to be closely graded; however, under normal circumstances a church had to have at least three hundred members before there were enough children for such a program. Automatically, with that kind of standard, the small church was a failure.

Often the assumption has been made that to do things right there has to be a critical mass of people of a particular age or sex or interest. Almost never are suggestions made about what is possible given varying numbers of people. When I have attempted to point out this problem, the response has typically been that I should be creative and able to adapt. It is difficult to fathom why a small-church pastor should be the one with all the creativity and ability to adapt, while resource-material producers have little of either.

In addition to size, a second factor is the difference in level of income. The small-church pastor compares the per capita giving in his or her church with the per capita giving in the large church. Look how much more Christian those people in the large church are! Why, they're giving twice as much per member as the people in the small church. No one bothers to point out that the average income in the large church may be three times that of the small church. When it comes to sacrificial giving, small-church members are frequently far ahead of the large church, but often all that is compared are the two per capita giving figures.

A third factor is the level of education. While there are variations, the level of education is often much higher in large urban and suburban churches than in small rural ones. A large proportion of college-educated people in a congregation provides a leadership group that is already trained to do many tasks. Many denominational Sunday school curricula seem to assume that teachers will have had a college education. Most of these curricula require a great deal of study and planning. Teachers need to be inner-directed and capable of sorting out and organizing what they will use. People with the required skills are more likely to be college educated than not. It is not surprising that denominationally approved Sunday school curricula are more widely used in large than in small churches.

Consider again the two churches mentioned above. The denomination launches a new curriculum. The pastor of the large church is soon telling about how enthusiastically his or her Sunday school teachers have accepted it and what a great curriculum it is. The pastor of the small church almost has a revolt on his or her hands. The teachers refuse to use the curriculum, complaining that it is too difficult. If the small-church pastor tries to convey to the denominational education staff these complaints, their reaction is often that there is nothing wrong with the curriculum. Rather, the teachers probably represent a fundamentalist backwash. The fact that the teachers in the large church are mostly college graduates and those in the small church are not is ignored.

A high level of education also means a large number of professionals, managers, and executives in the congregation. Such persons are much more likely to be problem solvers and accustomed to assuming and discharging responsibilities with little or no supervision than are people with less education and differing work experience. Also, such members may already possess skills that can be readily applied to jobs in the church. I am not suggesting a difference in *potential* leadership abilities; many noncollege-educated people are capable of carrying out complicated and sophisticated leadership tasks. The difference is that the large-church pastor often already has a leadership pool that can be tapped; the small-church pastor must develop the leadership potential in the congregation. This task of leadership development is often made even more difficult for the small-church pastor because he or she has little training for it, and most resource materials are not prepared with that circumstance in mind.

A fourth social factor is population change. For a number of years, especially during the greatest period of new church development, considerable attention was paid to churches that have grown from nothing to a thousand or more members. They were often held up as the example of what all churches should be. Many small churches were made to feel that they too could (and should) grow if they only had the evangelistic zeal of these successful congregations. It was seldom mentioned that these growing churches were in areas where there was a rapid increase in the number of potential members. Nor was mention made that many small churches were in areas of stable or declining population.

I have suggested some reasons that, especially among leaders, large churches often have more positive images than small ones. The image differences frequently are the result of social factors rather than of greater or lesser commitment. I may have overstated the comparisons since it is possible to point to many large churches that are currently in trouble due to other social factors and to many small churches that are very attractive; yet I believe that the situation I have described is generally accurate.

## Success As Measured by the New Testament

Large churches have been perceived as better and more desirable than small ones, especially small, rural congregations. Large churches can afford to pay their pastors more and are usually more willing to do so. Large churches are likely to have a pool of trained leaders. Large churches are more likely to have a significant number of professional people and executives whose life-styles and experiences are closer to those of educated ministers. Many pastors feel more at home with the well-educated than with others. In a society in which influence is based on bigness and money, large-church pastors naturally have more influence and status than their small-church colleagues. Large churches have usually been more profitable outlets in terms of mission dollars. In short, the large church approximates society's definition of success better than the small one.

In contrast with this popular standard of success is the New Testament concept of the wholeness of the system and the value of each part. St. Paul stressed this in 1 Corinthians 12:12–31, comparing the church to a body in which each part has an essential purpose. The body cannot function as intended if any part is missing or fails to fulfill its purpose. Thus it is foolish for one part of the body to disdain another because it is different or smaller.

St. Paul emphasized the necessity of evaluating each part of the body on the basis of the contribution it is designed to make and its fidelity to that purpose. It is not faulted for not fulfilling a function of some other part. It is foolish to condemn the ear because it cannot see or the eye because it cannot hear. The eye is to be judged by how faithfully it performs its function of seeing, and the ear on how faithfully it fulfills the function of hearing. As each part functions in its own way, the whole body is built up.

In a variety of ways, small and large churches are different. Each has its peculiar role to play in the ministry and mission of Christ's body in the world. Since each is faced with differing challenges and social settings (See chap. 3 for some implications of differing social settings for church functioning. ED.), no church is to be judged on the basis of its resemblance to another. It is to be judged on the fulfillment of its calling in light of its resources and setting. Each church, regardless of size, contributes to the life of the whole body of Christ. Neither the large nor small church need be ashamed of itself or judge itself or the other to be inferior.

This is a sound theological and sociological basis for evaluating churches of all sizes and for constructing our images of them.

## Some Positive Small-Church Images

It is time then to correct false images and to recognize the place and importance of small churches. We need realistic, positive expectations of what small churches can be and accomplish, but there is a danger in all this. Unrealistic positive images can do as much damage in the long run as false negative ones. We want not only positive but also *functional* images, what I have defined elsewhere as practical ideals:

A practical ideal is a mental picture, a conceptualization, a model, a dream, a vision of what a person or a group would like to see as truth or reality. This is how I wish the world or a piece of the world really was. A practical ideal has five characteristics.

First, it helps a person to deal with life as it is and does not cause him to flee from life.

Second, it has specific suggestions on how the present situation can be improved.

Third, it cannot be fully realized in this world.

Fourth, it makes it possible to measure accomplishments and distance.

Fifth, it feeds meaning back into the imperfect present.[2]

We need then practical ideals—realistic and functional images —when considering the small church. I would like to suggest four such images.

First, the small church can be a close, supportive fellowship in which people can develop commitment to one another because each can personally know all other members. Because people know one another well, each shares in the joys and sorrows of others. Their experiences provide a foundation for a meaningful fellowship. The celebration of communion provides a unique opportunity to symbolize and emphasize this fellowship. In a variety of ways the members have opportunities to appreciate the contributions each can make. By working together on various projects they develop a sense of oneness.

While a small church often experiences friction because people know one another too well, there can also be a close and supportive fellowship. Even in churches where there is conflict, beneath the surface there is a deep and genuine concern for one another. One of my failings as a young pastor was to see only the surface divisiveness and fail to realize that fellowship can grow even where there are differences. My task should have been to find ways to maximize the fellowship and minimize the divisiveness.

An abundance of resources can aid the minister and laypersons to realize this image of a close and supportive fellowship. The

New Testament, especially the writing of St. Paul, is full of help. There are books available on working with people and helping them to resolve their conflicts and work together.[3] Also, there are courses and workships on conflict resolution and community building. Though the small-church pastor or layperson who would give emphasis to this image of the church often has difficult problems to overcome, he or she also has great opportunities to build a sense of community in a world where it is often lacking.

A second practical ideal for the small church is that the minister make the pastoral task the major vehicle for his or her ministry, the image of the shepherd who knows all the sheep and is aware when one is missing. In the small church the pastor can have meaningful, ongoing personal relationships with every member, knowing each one's strengths and weaknesses. Furthermore, he or she can have more personal influence on all members than is possible in the large church. The development of relationships is as important as, or more important than, the development of programs, which is a supplement to and supporter of relationships. Administration and organization can be part of the total work of the small-church pastor who emphasizes the pastoral task.

In discussing the different roles of pastors in the small and the large church, I do not imply that one is better than the other. In each situation there are unique advantages (and disadvantages).

Third, the small church provides opportunity for the full development of each person's potential and for adequate recognition of each one's contribution. It is important for the pastor to be able to assess members' abilities and appreciate the constraints that education and culture place on them. If a pastor can do this and also develop the ability to be a teacher and facilitator, he or she can have a meaningful ministry and see the fruits of his or her labor.

Fourth, the small church, especially one in a rural area, offers the pastor and congregation unique opportunities to be community leaders. The more rural the setting, the more important the church as a significant community institution. The pastor in a rural church is almost automatically a community leader.

Several years ago a state university embarked on a program of rural community development in its service area. It was not successful until its leaders recognized that it was essential to enlist the support of the churches, particularly the pastors.

About 1900, some people began realizing that the way land was being used was wrong. Timber cutters denuded hillsides, leaving the soil to be washed away. Poor planting methods led to massive erosion in which thousands of acres became useless. Out of this recognition grew the conservation movement in which rural ministers and laity played an important role. They stressed that we are called to be stewards of the soil. Soil Stewardship Sunday became an important celebration in the rural church calendar. Over a period of years the attitude of many farmers toward the use of land was radically changed.[4]

Whatever the status of churches and ministers in our society as a whole, it is safe to say that both are highly valued in rural areas. Opportunities for vital community leadership are open to churches and ministers and can be effectively met when ministers and laity understand how to be effective change agents.

In these and other ways, small churches can develop realistic and functional images that enable them to be faithful parts of Christ's body and to contribute to his continuing ministry and mission.

## Conclusion

As an important part of the church system, small churches have significant contributions to make; they offer opportunities for meaningful ministries. Because of this they deserve the best leadership the church can provide. Since this is often young and inexperienced leadership, the church must do everything possible to support it so that ministries will be constructive and young ministers will have positive learning experiences. People should see small churches as opportunities for ministry and not as steppingstones to something better or as necessary evils. It should be recognized that the skilled small-church pastor is as competent as any· other minister. Let the church judge, not as the world judges, but as God judges. Out of these Nazareths, too, can come something good.

## NOTES

1. See Robert Rosenthal and Lenore Jacobson, *Pygmalion in the Classroom* (New York: Holt, Rinehart & Winston, 1968).

2. Arthur C. Tennies, *A Church for Sinners, Seekers, and Sunday Non-Saints* (Nashville: Abingdon Press, 1974), pp. 139 ff.

3. See, for example, Speed Leas and Paul Kittlaus, *Church Fights, Managing Conflict in the Local Church* (Philadelphia: Westminster Press, 1973).

4. Ironically, this contribution has not always been acknowledged or appreciated. A report of a meeting of a group of scholars (*New York Times*, 1 May, 1974) indicated the scholars' sharp critique of the traditional Christian attitude toward nature as contributing to environmental destruction. While they were partly correct, they failed to appreciate the important contributions that small rural congregations have made to the sense of stewardship of natural resources. This seems to be another example of negative images blocking appreciation of the positive features and contributions of small churches.

# 5

# The Ordained Clergy
# in Small Congregations

*Jackson W. Carroll and James C. Fenhagen*

"Let your bearing towards one another arise out of your life in Christ Jesus," wrote St. Paul to the church in Philippi (Phil. 2:5, N&B). Paul touched the heart of Christian ministry: a calling to authenticity through which the life-giving power of the risen Christ is communicated from one person to another. The unique opportunity of the ordained ministry in a small congregation lies in the regular and potentially intimate contacts which make authenticity possible. The ministry to the small congregation, therefore, is a special vocation requiring particular skills. For many it is a life of deep personal satisfaction, but it is also a ministry confronted with particular difficulties.

In the state of Maine "Rev. Sam Blank" (a name we will use for a composite of several ministers we have met) is the pastor of two churches located in communities about fifteen miles apart. Many years ago the smaller of the two communities was a thriving railroad center, providing support for the lumber industry. With the modernization of the railroad, this once proud town began to die, and this unspoken fact, more than anything else, dominates the mood and aspirations of the people who live there. The second community is a town of twenty-five hundred people within commuting distance of one of Maine's larger cities. It is agriculturally oriented, with a small shoe factory as its only industry. There has been slow but noticeable growth over the past fifteen years which, among other things, has contributed to a spirit of vitality and optimism in the lives of its people.

Sam Blank chose to work in these two communities. He lives in the second of the two and, as a young man six years out of seminary, finds friendship among the people he serves. He is quite frank to admit his preference. The mood of the dying community affects him; the feeling of vitality and health in the community where he lives is reflected in the way he describes his ministry. "The biggest thing I find personally is that people are willing to let you be who you are," he says. "I think this is because the congregation and community are so small. I see the people there as people rather than parishioners."

His frustrations revolve around issues of isolation, feelings of powerlessness, and lack of resources. "Our town is having a terrible time maintaining our hospital," Mr. Blank points out. "The standards of the federal government are geared to the city hospital. We are utterly powerless." This sense of powerlessness, he notes, spills over into every aspect of community life, including of course the church.

Mr. Blank finds his ministry rewarding because it provides daily contact with people in a variety of circumstances and from a variety of backgrounds. "I know most everybody in the county," he says. "It's a good feeling to walk down the street and have at least a nodding acquaintance with most everyone I see." Sam has a natural warmth to which people respond, but he admits to a need for strengthening his counseling skills. "I do a lot of counseling," he says, "not because I'm the greatest counselor in the world, but because there are not many of us around to whom people can come." He mentions a similar need for skills relating to the building of community. "I wish I knew more about how to deal with conflict situations. It seems that the more often people see one another—as is the case in a small church—the easier it is to get their backs up about something." The skills necessary for an effective ministry in the small congregation were not part of seminary training. They are, however, skills that can be learned.

When Sam Blank speaks of the personal satisfaction in his ministry, he is enthusiastic. When pressed, however, he can also speak of isolation and loneliness. His greatest support is his wife who is also deeply involved in the lives of the two churches. She shares his enthusiasm most of the time but feels the weight of being Sam's major source of support. "There are times when I feel lonely too, and Sam doesn't always understand this. I don't want to be his cheerleader."

The hardest question Sam Blank must answer has to do with his future plans. "Sam, if you were called to a large church in a city or suburban community, would you go?" he was asked. There was a long and thoughtful pause.

"In all honesty, if the situation were right, I guess I would." Not all clergy in small congregations would agree with Sam Blank. For some, the rewards of serving in a small church are special and the effort eminently worthwhile. They understand their vocation as a call to serve in small churches.

Regardless of the position they take concerning their careers, small-church clergy face some distinctive opportunities and issues. To describe more fully the characteristics and situations of ministers in small congregations, and to supplement the information in the case of Sam Blank, we have drawn on data from a 1968 survey of Protestant clergy.[1] In analyzing the survey responses for our purposes, we compared clergy serving one or more congregations, the largest of which did not exceed two hundred members, with clergy in congregations of more than two hundred members. Additionally, we compared the responses of small-church clergy according to the location of their parishes (town and country, small city, suburban, and large city). Drawing on these data we first present a brief profile of some personal and social characteristics of small-church ministers. We also use the data to gain some insight into their roles as ministers of small congregations. After these essentially descriptive concerns, we turn to three important issues facing small-church ministers—career lines, rewards, and support—which we believe need to be addressed for the sake of the ministers of small congregations.

### Small-Church Clergy: Who Are They and What Do They Do?

#### Personal and Social Characteristics

Who are typical small-church clergy? While they are spread across a wide age-range, the modal age category of clergy serving small churches is the thirty-to-thirty-nine-year-old group (31 percent). When compared to the age distribution of clergy in larger congregations, small-church clergy are significantly more likely to be in the youngest (under thirty) and oldest (over sixty) age groups. Thus, small churches are likely to be served by either recent entrants into the ministry or persons nearing retirement, to be entry and exit points for many ministerial careers.

The clergy responding to the survey were overwhelmingly male, as might be expected; thus, we have no data on women clergy. A dramatic increase in the number of women attending seminary has occurred since the 1968 survey. We suspect that they, like most male seminary graduates, will initially serve small congregations. However, we also suspect that sexism in assignment or calling practices in the church may mean that women clergy will not find "promotion" to large congregations as easy as it is for their male counterparts. Thus women clergy of all ages may increasingly be found in small congregations.

Although nonwhites were a part of the survey, there were too few to constitute a representative group. Nevertheless, of nonwhite clergy in the study, the largest proportion are serving small congregations, and most of these are in churches in urban settings.

In educational background, small-church clergy, like their larger-church counterparts, are typically seminary graduates (47 percent and 50 percent respectively) with an additional 27 percent and 40 percent respectively reporting postseminary graduate work. However, four times as many small-church clergy (16 percent) report college graduation or less as their highest educational level as compared with larger-church clergy (4 percent). Of those clergy who attended seminary, the large majority received their education for ministry in a seminary of their own denomination. Seven percent more small-church than large-church clergy report having been trained in a Bible college or institute (9 percent and 2 percent respectively).

The large majority of all clergy in the sample are married. Likewise a significant number of all clergy (58 percent) report that their wives are employed and receive money income. Congregational size, however, seems to make a significant difference in the reasons given for the wife's working. Wives of small-church clergy are considerably more likely (by 15 percent) than wives of clergy in larger congregations to be working primarily because of insufficient family income to meet expenses. Almost 53 percent are in this category. They are less likely (by 12 percent) to be working to pay for their children's education. Roughly similar proportions report that their wives work to fulfill their training or special interests (about 17 percent) or because of a need for an additional challenge beyond homemaking (10 percent).

## Context and Role

The brief view of Sam Blank's ministry highlights several aspects of his role as minister in a small congregation—the opportunity for a very personal ministry, demands for counseling, and need for particular skills such as conflict management. To what extent is his case typical? Are there unique aspects of small churches and their contexts that make ministry in them different? Our survey data do not give a full picture, but they provide some answers.

Clergy were asked to describe (in an open-ended question) the aspect of ministry to which they devote an unusual amount of time and energy. The responses were grouped into several categories. Differences are small between small- and larger-church clergy. The largest proportion of each group reported spending most time and effort in the area of local church life (a general ministry category that includes worship, preaching, stewardship, administration, youth work, and so on). Counseling and pastoral care, including visitation and work with the elderly, is the second most-chosen category for both groups, followed by educational activities and community social action. The functional demands on ministers in the two types of churches do not seem to be very different.

When responses of small-church clergy alone are examined in terms of church location, several significant differences may be noted. Pastors in rural areas are most likely (27 percent) to designate local church life as their primary ministry area, as are also suburban clergy (20 percent); this is second in importance for urban and small-city clergy. Both urban and small-city clergy (23 percent and 29 percent respectively) list counseling and pastoral care as their primary functions. This category is second in importance for rural and suburban clergy. For all but urban clergy, educational concerns are third in importance. Only 5 percent of the urban clergy rate education as primary, possibly reflecting a relative absence of children and youth in small urban congregations. For urban clergy, approximately 18 percent indicate community social action as their primary area of functioning as compared with 11 percent for rural, 6 percent for suburban, and 5 percent for small-city clergy. Missions and evangelism is the fifth most important category for rural clergy (9 percent), and the category is chosen by 8 percent of the suburban, 6 percent of the small-city, and 4 percent of the urban clergy.

These data, especially the importance of the "local church life" category, reflect the generalist orientation required of most small-church clergy. Such an orientation is necessitated by budgetary constraints and by the absence in many cases of available clergy specialists or trained lay leadership. For some small clergy, the opportunity to specialize and secure the assistance of other specialists is being opened through team ministries and cooperative parish structures.

The importance also of pastoral concerns—visiting and counseling—for many small-church clergy reflects the emphasis in an earlier study of rural clergy respondents on the minister's concern for people. One of the ministers wrote: "Ministers succeed or fail . . . not on their ability to preach, nor on their knowledge of history; not on their Biblical understanding, nor any of the scholarly matters, but on their ability to effectively communicate a Christian concern for people."[2]

The relative importance of community social action for urban small-church clergy no doubt reflects in part the influence of setting. Small urban congregations are typically found in inner-city and transitional neighborhoods. Once much larger, they have lost members to suburban flight. They may now serve specialized constituencies, such as the elderly who stayed behind or the racial or ethnic newcomers who moved in as old residents left. The needs of such specialized congregations or of the larger neighborhood may lead clergy into social-action-oriented ministries.

We also note, as the Sam Blank case suggests, that the "person" of the minister, especially in rural and small-town areas, is often a more important factor in his or her functioning in church and community settings than is competence in one or more of the practitioner roles. Because of the opportunity for close interpersonal relations which small congregations allow, and because of the high social visibility of the minister in rural areas and small towns, as Vidich and Bensman note, "People take an interest in his public behavior and in his private life and judge him on the basis of his personality and how he 'fits' into the life of the community."[3]

In several ways, then, context and size of the congregation interact to affect the role and functioning of clergy in small (and large) congregations.

If clergy, small- and large-church alike, are to function effectively in their roles, there is need, as Sam Blank recognized, for continuing professional development. The growth of such opportunities and the response to them has been considerable in recent years. Our 1968 data show that a sizeable number of clergy engaged in one or more continuing education experiences (of longer than three days) during the year of the survey. Sixty percent of the total sample of parish clergy were involved in one or more such experiences. A more recent follow-up study by Robert Bonn[4] shows the rate of participation in continuing education to have increased to 67 percent. The size of the church had little influence on participation. There were no significant differences in types of continuing education programs pursued by the two types of pastors. In 1974, professional skills (preaching, group work, counseling, planning) attracted the greatest interest. Where significant differences between small- and large-church clergy are evident is in the amount of financial support available for continuing education. If small-church clergy receive the lowest salaries, as the data show, they also receive the least extra financial assistance for their continuing education. This is an illustration of the inadequate reward and support systems which the small-church minister typically experiences.

## Issues Facing Small-Church Clergy

**Career**

In their historical treatment of small congregations in chapter 1, Robert Lynn and James Fraser note a profound shift in the concept of a professional that occurred in the early nineteenth century. The notion of entering a career was introduced, and career implied a ladder to be climbed toward greater success in one's profession. Furthermore, success was practically synonymous with bigness. For the minister, career success came to mean moving from smaller to larger churches. That this "ladder" model of a career is still with us as a broad cultural norm may be seen in a recent description of an occupational career: "Entry into a position that requires the performance of occupational duties at the *lowest rung of the occupational ladder.* This is followed by a *sequence of promotions into higher-level positions* within an organization, leading eventually to the *pinnacle*, and finally to retirement."[5] While many individuals fail to conform to this model, it is probably true that the career model is a value-laden cultural expectation that most persons bring to occupations, including the ministry.

Sam Blank is no exception. He admits to the "pull" of a larger congregation. The survey data also suggest that this is the case generally. We found no significant differences between small- and large-church clergy in general satisfaction with the ministry as a profession. Approximately 56 percent of both groups report high satisfaction, with an additional 33 to 55 percent reporting moderate satisfaction. Significant differences, however, are evident in the degree of satisfaction with present congregations. Small-church clergy are more likely to report dissatisfaction with their present congregations and are more likely to be actively seeking changes in position. While the data do not indicate what their change aspirations are, we strongly suspect that they involve larger congregations, as was the case for Sam Blank.

Lest we give the impression that the desire for career mobility is simply a matter of status striving by individual clergy, we wish to emphasize that it is a structural aspect of denominational life. Built into the informal and, often, formal operational policies of most denominations are expectations and mechanisms that support career ladders.

This often begins in seminary, if not earlier. Successful clergy invited to join seminary faculties, usually in the practical fields, have almost always come from large churches where the bigger-is-better image prevails. Their teaching of the practice of ministry is typically slanted in the direction of the large church rather than toward the small one. Additionally, when seminarians must work to support their education, they frequently serve as ministers of small congregations unable to afford full-time ministers. Yet these ministry experiences in small churches are rarely taken seriously by the seminary as opportunities for disciplined reflection on the practice of ministry. The assumption seems to be that viable ministry cannot really occur in such contexts. The overall message that is communicated and reinforced through these and other seminary experiences is that ministry occurs most authentically in larger churches.

The situation does not change when the seminarian graduates and, as our data show, typically is assigned or called to a small congregation as his or her first parish. It soon becomes apparent that clergy who hold visible positions in conference, presbytery, or diocesan affairs are those who have "made it" to the larger churches. They are invited to give the addresses and chair important committees; such clergy become reference groups, if not role models, for the young minister. Watching them, he or she learns the game of jovial jockeying for positions. This seduction often occurs in spite of the idealism and antiestablishment posture the young person brings to ministry. For the effective minister, the seduction is reinforced by parishioners who worry aloud "how long we'll be able to keep our minister before some large congregation hears about him or her and extends a call."

Denominational policies regarding clergy deployment vary sufficiently to make it difficult to generalize about their support for career ladders promoting upward mobility. The appointive system of the United Methodist Church, for instance, has policies which clearly support such ladders, and this is the case in varying degrees in other denominations.

We are aware, however, that there is not one career ladder in a denomination, but several. Some reach higher than others, and some seem more horizontal than vertical. James Lowery speculates that there are two definite career tracks in the Episcopal church. One involves churches of two hundred members or less and an annual budget of less than twenty thousand dollars. He suggests that one either moves off this track within the first two to three years of ordination or stays in that slot most of one's active ministry. He further estimates that over 40 percent of the Episcopal clergy fail to move off this track but spend their entire career serving churches in this category.[6]

Why some make the higher ladder and others do not is only partly the result of ability or motivation. It may also be caused by a variety of factors, including complex issues of supply and demand, having attended the "right" seminary, having a prominent minister for a father or sponsor early in one's career. These various career advantages have been called by some[7] the "Matthew effect": "For to everyone who has will more be given, and he will have in abundance; but from him who has not, even what he has will be taken away" (Matt. 25:29).

What can be done to break the hold of the "bigger equals better" image of career success? There are obviously no easy methods of fighting a deeply engrained cultural value that extends far beyond the church and is supported by institutionalized policies and procedures. Nevertheless, some steps seem possible.

First, a program of consciousness raising like that which blacks and women have experienced is essential. Theological faculties and seminarians, denominational officials, clergy, and laity need to become aware that "small is beautiful" and conscious of the detrimental and often dehumanizing ways in which formal and informal policies and procedures support the "bigger is better" notion.

Consciousness raising alone is inadequate. Changes are needed in denominational policies and procedures. Reward and support systems are two areas that may be changed to reduce the lure of the large church. It is also important that the context for ministry in small congregations be enhanced. Some small congregations have such a low regard for themselves and for their possibilities for ministry that they provide strong impetus for their clergy to mount the career ladder. The development of trained lay leadership (see chap. 6) and imaginative programming (see chap. 7) are ways of making small congregations more desirable contexts for rewarding, long-term clergy tenures.

### Rewards

One of the ways in which the career ladder—so detrimental to small congregations—is supported is through rewarding ministry positions unequally according to size of congregation. That this is the case is clear from our survey data.

Though it comes as no surprise, there are large salary differentials between clergy in small congregations and those in larger ones. Seventy-eight percent of small-church clergy reported total cash salaries in 1968 of less than $6,000. Less than half (31 percent) of the large-church pastors reported figures as low. Small-church pastors in town and country areas had a median salary of $5,580. In small cities the median salary of small-church pastors was $6,940; in suburbs it was $7,616; and in large cities it was

$7,328. In each case substantially higher salaries were received in the larger churches.

Related to the salary issue, twice as many small-church clergy (16 percent) report holding second jobs as is true for those in larger churches. In a 1974 survey of clergy, the percentage of moonlighting among all clergy increased significantly over 1968. The median congregational size for clergy moonlighting less than twenty hours per week is 245 members, and these churches are typically in nonrural areas. The median church size of those reporting more than twenty hours of secular employment per week is 124 members, and these churches are typically located in rural areas.[9]

Small-church clergy are significantly less likely than larger-church clergy (39 percent and 50 percent respectively) to have annual salary reviews. They are also considerably less likely to have received raises over the preceding five years.

Such salary differentials, as well as low clergy salaries in general, lead to dissatisfaction. Small-church clergy are significantly more likely than larger-church clergy to agree that their salaries are too low to meet family needs and too low in comparison to comparably educated professionals. Both groups of clergy strongly affirm these statements. However, small-church clergy are considerably more likely (51 percent to 33 percent) to believe that their salaries are too low as compared with those of fellow clergy in their denominations.

The salary issue is serious. Several strategies are being tried with varying degrees of success. Salary equilization plans, with increments for years of service, family size, educational needs, and so on have been proposed and occasionally tried but have not proved successful as far as is known. Various alternatives to direct salary payments are often used by congregations (and/or clergy) as a means of circumventing the plan.

In lieu of salary equilization, many denominations establish minimum salary plans and provide supplements when congregations cannot afford to pay the minimum. This, however, raises the serious question of where assistance leaves off and dependence begins.

A strategy increasingly gaining legitimacy in some denominations is that of nonstipendiary or "tentmaking ministries," where the minister supplements ministry income with a secular job. It is obviously not a new strategy, and it is fairly widely practiced, as indicated by the data cited above on moonlighting. What is relatively new is its acceptance and encouragement by some denominations and congregations. In order to guarantee that its minister receive an adequate salary, one congregation arranged as part of the call to share its minister with a community welfare agency. In another instance, the minister serves as chaplain to a textile mill, the town's only industry. The issue of nonstipendiary clergy, however, is delicate, working best when the "secular" ministry and the ministry to a congregation bear some similarity. Where this is not the case, there is the real risk of competition between jobs and wasted energy.

We are now in an era of tighter and tighter financial resources. Many congregations will close, some of necessity, some out of sheer unwillingness to experiment with new alternatives. At the Hartford Seminary Foundation we have been working with the Berkshire Association of the United Church of Christ (Massachusetts) in developing an intensive two-year program that will prepare laity to serve effectively as lay pastors. In other areas we are seeing the emergence of "sacramentalists" and the ordination of community leaders who will function as pastors in their churches. The possibilities are numerous when the soil has been carefully and lovingly tilled.

Salary, however, is not the only way ministry positions are rewarded. Both power and psychic gratification are additional important and necessary rewards. Power is the opportunity to have a voice in shaping the policies and practices of the system in which a person is active. Psychic gratification is the reward of feeling needed, appreciated, and recognized for one's accomplishments. On both accounts small-church clergy (and often also the congregations in which they serve) are typically underrewarded. Denominations have not found adequate means of providing either of these rewards in satisfactory ways. One need not attend many gatherings of small-church clergy before one hears expressions of pain, frustration, and lack of power.

Gaining power to have a voice in policies that affect one's situation has been partly facilitated by some denominations' attempts at reorganization to allow for more grass roots participation. Where this is insufficient, small-church clergy and laity need to become proactive on behalf of their concerns. In one area, small-church clergy and laity have organized themselves as a coalition to insure participation and power in denominational planning and policy making. A variety of issues affect their lives around which coalitions may be formed to secure a hearing.

In addition to gaining power, small churches need to be acknowledged by the church at large as a significant part of the church's life, and their clergy and laity need to be recognized as contributors to the life of the church. In one denominational jurisdiction, experienced pastors in small congregations have formed a team responsible for training younger clergy. As part of this team, they are given ongoing training in order to do the best job possible. As a result they are seen and acknowledged by others for their talents.

The development of the team-ministry concept has also done much to recognize individual gifts, although with some obvious difficulties. One cluster of churches has developed a plan to call to their area pastors with quite diverse but distinctive skills. In addition to ability in the overall ministry of the parish, one minister was a trained pastoral counselor, another a youth worker, another an educator. Under this arrangement, each church in the cluster was free to draw on the talents it needed. The clergy were recognized for the skills they genuinely possessed and were challenged to grow by the jobs they were being called on to do. The difficulties developed around the strong feelings each congregation had for a "minister of their own," resenting the time when the specialty seemed to get in the way.

Recognition and reward are major factors in career development. They affect both mobility and morale. There is a genuine need to address them on a large scale and to develop strategies that will provide the church with new alternatives for a critical problem.

### Support

In addition to the issues of career ladders and rewards, support looms large as an issue for clergy in small churches. No one can function effectively without genuine support. It has nothing to do with whether a person is strong or weak, at his or her creative best, or in serious trouble. Support implies that network of authentic relationships we need in order to function effectively. "Support," as Dr. Gerald Caplan points out, "is an enduring pattern of continuous or intermittent ties that can be spontaneous or highly organized, but in either case serves to validate our personal identity and worth, provides genuine help with the work we are engaged in, and responds to our overall need to be dealt with as an unique individual."[10]

Although our survey data contain no information regarding these issues, problems of isolation and lack of intellectual stimulation occur over and over again in conversations with clergy located in largely rural areas. Clergy in urban congregations generally have the stimulation they need, but they experience isolation in other ways. For married clergy, the family is generally experienced as a primary source of support. If this is the only system of support, however, there is the danger of real difficulty. One problem of mobility is the strain placed on the family to respond to more needs than it is capable of meeting.

The traditional denominational structures—associations, deaneries, districts, and the like—were undoubtedly created with concern for support in mind. In times past, and even in some cases today, these structures fill the bill. However, in most cases they do not because built into them all are problems of competitiveness, individualism, and career-success striving that plague the ministry and make support so difficult.

Genuine support is not a luxury but a fundamental element in the professional and personal growth of anyone who takes life seriously. The word *support*, therefore, does not mean "propping up" someone who is in danger of falling down, but rather in Caplan's words, "the augmenting of a person's strengths to facilitate his or her mastering of the environment."[11] Support in this sense is as necessary for the personal and professional growth of the minister as is prayer.

Two approaches to the question of support are currently receiving a good deal of attention across the church. The first is the development of Colleague Groups (support groups), and the second, the development of a more mutual ministry between clergy and laity that can provide genuine support within the parish setting. Neither of these approaches is particularly new, but each is an attempt to make support or genuine mutuality normative in the life of the church.

The term *Colleague Groups* implies more than a casual meeting of friends or a monthly get-together of the local minister's association. It is a group of from six to fifteen persons who meet on a regular basis around a clear set of expectations. Generally, the meetings are at least every three weeks, and they involve a disciplined agenda, including a balance between personal and professional concerns. A typical colleague-group meeting might include time for personal sharing, Bible study, a case study on a particular issue in the ministry of one of the members, or a presentation of subject matter having to do with the practice of ministry.

Mark Rouch, of Interpreter's House in North Carolina, has done extremely creative work in fostering a colleague-group network in which information is shared and resources are provided, including telephone linkages with other networks. Duane Meyer in Iowa has developed a taped cassette program to enable support groups to develop and to assist in developing their agendas. In 1967, Eugene Timmons began with his Presbytery in Kansas to develop a training program for colleague group leaders, which includes a highly disciplined system of supervision. The Hartford Seminary Foundation has been working in similar fashion, and undoubtedly the success of the Academy of Parish Clergy rests largely in the seriousness with which the Academy has addressed this issue.[12] No one can function effectively without adequate support. This is the key to a creative and consistent ministry in the small church.

The development of mutual ministry within the parish approaches the need for support from a different perspective. The theological conviction underlying it is that all baptized persons have been given a ministry. The task of the church is to enable these ministries to be carried out and to provide the support necessary to sustain them. The primary ministry of the ordained person is to the congregation. If this ministry is to be effective, he or she needs the support of at least a few members of the laity on a consistent basis. In the same manner, the laity need the support of the clergy (and other laity) in the exercise of their ministry. Again, we mean more than a good word now and then, or even the willingness to pitch in and help out. Mutual support means a disciplined sharing of concerns, honest feedback, and, most importantly, the willingness to share one another's particular journeys in faith. Such mutuality is not easy. As one lay person stated quite clearly, "I don't want to hear my minister talk about his struggles and doubts. I want him to be a spiritual leader." Or, as a minister expressed, "Quite frankly, I find it difficult to share my personal faith with anyone. Being a teacher can be a protection."

Both of these statements touch issues that lie at the heart of mutuality. Mutuality for Christians can only begin as we learn what it means at the deepest level to "be present" to one another. When this happens, the seed of genuine support has been planted.

In ·Sam Blank's ministry, the greatest support came from his wife and family. There is a limit, however, to the family's role. Support involves both personal and professional growth. The need is for a network of support, self-consciously developed to meet a variety of needs. Often clergy wait passively for support, hoping it will suddenly appear from nowhere. A support network does not just happen; it is carefully and lovingly developed. When it is not present, the denomination is responsible for helping it happen. Where there is a network of genuine support, there is the possibility of a vital and effective ministry in the smallest of congregations. But, unfortunately, despite all the talk about support in the past few years, networks of genuine support are still a rarity.

In this chapter, of necessity, we have had to be selective in both the descriptive data and the issues we have considered. Nevertheless, we believe these issues are crucial and need urgently and imaginatively to be addressed for the sake of Sam Blank, his fellow clergy (both men and women), and the small congregations they serve. The challenge presented to the small church is a challenge to the church-at-large "to equip God's people for work in his service, to the building up of the body of Christ" (Eph. 4:12, NEB).

## NOTES

1. In preparing this chapter, we had access to data from a 1968 study of clergy compensation undertaken by Dr. Edgar W. Mills, then director of the Ministry Studies Board. The survey utilized questionnaires mailed to a randomly selected sample of 7990 clergy in 21 Protestant denominations in the United States. A response rate of

approximately 58 percent was achieved. More detailed information regarding the survey is reportd in Edgar W. Mills and Janet F. Morse, "Clergy Support in 1968, Income and Attitudes," *Spectrum/Journal* (January–February, 1970), pp. 19–26.

2. Samuel W. Blizzard, "The Roles of the Rural Parish Minister, The Protestant Seminaries, and the Sciences of Social Behavior," *The Sociology of Religion, An Anthology,* ed. Richard D. Knudten (New York: Appleton-Century-Crofts, 1967), p. 246.

3. Arthur J. Vidich and Joseph Bensman, *Small Town in Mass Society* (Garden City, N.Y.: Doubleday Anchor Books, 1958), p. 244.

4. Robert L. Bonn, *Containing Education Participants: Who, How Many, Types of Program* (Richmond, Va.: Society for the Advancement of Continuing Education for Ministry, 1975).

5. Walter L. Slocum, *Occupational Careers* (Chicago: Aldine, 1974), p. 5, italics ours.

6. James Lowery, Jr., *Peers, Tents, and Owls, Some Solutions to Problems of Clergy Today* (New York: Morehouse-Barlow, 1973), pp. 89–90.

7. See Robert Merton, "The Matthew Effect in Science," *Science* (January 1968), pp. 56–63.

8. Mills and Morse, "Clergy Support in 1968."

9. Robert L. Bonn, "Moonlighting Clergy," *The Christian Ministry,* (September 1975), pp. 4–8.

10. Quoted by David Richards, "Support Systems," (n.d.). Available from the Office of Pastoral Development, 116 Alhambra Circle, Coral Gables, Florida.

11. Ibid.

12. Addresses for contacting the persons or programs mentioned in this paragraph are: Dr. Mark Rouch, Interpreter's House, Lake Junaluska, N.C. 29745; Rev. Duane Meyer, Iowa Conference of the United Church of Christ, 600 42nd St., Des Moines, Iowa 50312; Rev. Eugene Timmons, Director, Judicatory Career Support System, 3501 Campbell, Kansas City, Mo. 64109; Hartford Seminary Foundation, 55 Elizabeth St., Hartford, Ct. 06105; Academy of Parish Clergy, 3100 West Lake St., Minneapolis, Minn. 55416.

# 6

# Shared Ministry: Lay Leadership Development

*Richard E. Colby and Charity Waymouth*

The purpose of this chapter is to explore the meaning of the phrase *shared ministry* and to suggest some ways to identify, validate, and further develop effective participation in ministry by lay people in the church. The first section deals with the basic meaning of the phrase, and the second suggests some actions that can begin to implement the sharing of ministry within the local church community. We are not naive about some of the obstacles that these clarifications and suggested actions will create in any one denomination because of tradition, present practices, and existing structures. These obstacles may arise from interpretation of traditional language, present roles of clergy and lay people, or the way the life of a congregation is currently ordered. They should not, however, deter people from acting on what they believe in order that growth can take place in the Christian community and their mission to serve the Lord Jesus Christ as his church in the world can be accomplished. We hope that these obstacles, when confronted openly, honestly, and through the power of the Holy Spirit, can provide fresh opportunities to respond anew to the gospel message. A careful reading of history documents that this process—acting out basic beliefs—has been part of the individual Christian experience. It has also both the experience of the collective body of Christ as both have struggled to live out the commands of the gospel since the beginning of the church in New Testament times.

## Definition of Ministry

What do we mean by *shared ministry*? According to the earliest sources, the *ministry* of the church is the "work" of the Christian community. This work is a natural action (serving) that grows out of faith (believing) in the life and work of the person of Jesus Christ. Basically, ministry is an active response to our faith in Jesus Christ, whether the responding is done individually as one member of the body or collectively as the community of believers.

In discussing ministry in the primitive church, John Knox made the following observations:

> When Paul gives us the first account we possess of the various functions being performed by individuals in the primitive church (1 Cor. 12:4–30), he speaks of them as "varieties of ministries." He can refer to himself and to other workers as "ministers" of the new covenant, or of Christ, or of God, or of the church, or of the gospel, or simply as "ministers," and to their work as a "ministry of reconciliation" (2 Cor. 3:6, 11:23; Col. 1:7, 25, 4:7; 2 Cor. 5:18; etc.). . . . The word [ministry], whether in Greek or English, simply means "service;" and although it soon came to stand for a particular ecclesiastical office, the office of the deacon, its original more inclusive sense was never completely lost.[1]

Ministry then, in the fundamental sense, implies work that is done by those who believe, their service to one another and to the world around them that members of the Christian community perform in the name of Christ because they believe in him.

In 1 Corinthians 12, two important facts about ministry become evident. First, this work is part of the life experience of *everyone* who believes. "There are varieties of gifts, but the same Spirit. There are varieties of service, but the same Lord. There are many forms of work, but all of them, in all men, are the work of the same God. In each of us the Spirit is manifested in one particular way, for some useful purpose" (1 Cor. 12:4–7, NEB). Everyone who believes is involved in these actions of service; indeed, the power of the Spirit is shown forth in distinct ways in each of us. God does not work only through a few, nor should the work that is accomplished in his name be expressed through the lives of just a few. The Spirit is present and active in each one who believes and must be shown forth in service, in ministry.

The second fact evident from Paul's words to the Corinthians is that this work is for some useful purpose. There is some reason for this action which is useful to the health and life of the church and its mission to the world. Ministry is the responsibility of everyone, and when the work force, so to speak, is reduced in any way, the usefulness of the believing community will be reduced. Paul said, "For Christ is like a single body with its many limbs and organs, which, many as they are, together make up one body" (1 Cor. 12:12, NEB). The human body functions most usefully when each part performs the purpose for which it was created. Christ's body, the church, functions most usefully when each believer responds to the Spirit and fulfills the purpose for which he or she was created.

## Dimensions of Shared Ministry

This basic definition of ministry—the work of all who believe in Jesus Christ—evolves out of our belief and is useful and necessary for the health and life of the whole church, the body of Christ. What dimensions are added when we speak of *shared* ministry? First, the ministry can and should be part of each believer's life. In his recent book, *The Future Shape of the Ministry,* Urban T. Holmes, III, says, "Most lay people consider themselves the recipients of ministry and consequently there is little sense of lay apostolate."[2] The problem arises, not only through the perception of lay people, but as Holmes documents further: "To put the same thing another way, in the minds of many churchmen, the Church's ministry is gathered up in one office represented by the local pastor."[3]

In a recent conversation, a clergyperson identified the same issue in stating that most clergy see the word *minister* as a verb while most lay people think of the word as a noun. However the dilemma is articulated, the reality is that ministry is not seen as the work of all who believe but as the work of a few—the clergy. Even when we refer to lay ministry, the temptation is to speak of lay people doing the work that is usually seen as the job of the minister. In a recent report of the findings of a task force assessing the needs of small congregations, lay ministry is described as follows: "This is where a lay person is called to fulfill specific functions within the congregation, ordinarily performed by the clergy."[4] Consequently, when we talk about shared ministry, it is easy to assume that we are talking about other people sharing the ministry of the clerical person. Many lay persons have been frustrated in their attempts to respond to ministry in their lives by trying to emulate the pastor and feeling that they do not have the skills and the talents to do what he or she does.

We need desperately, for the sake of clergy and lay persons alike, to reaffirm the principle that ministry, the work of the church, not only can, but must be part of the life of each Christian, whether trained to perform a specific function or not. In the preface of *Learning to Share the Ministry,* Loren Mead of the Alban Institute discusses the experiences of one congregation:

I have seen ordinary folk who go to a congregation get turned on to what the gospel means in their community and to them personally, and I have seen them invent new paths of mission and ministry. . . . It doesn't happen when people try to copy other people. It doesn't happen when people try to get somebody else to tell them what to do. It starts happening when people start saying, "This ministry is *mine*. What happens for Christ in this parish somehow depends on me, on us."[5]

This process of identifying ministry as part of the life of each believer will not happen automatically. Too many conditioned experiences within the life of the church reinforce the idea that ministry evolves only from the office of the ordained minister. It will happen only when Christian people, ordained and not ordained, make honest efforts to reaffirm what the gospel states: that the Spirit is in each of us working for some useful purpose.

Second, when ministry is seen as a shared experience, there is the need to encourage people to identify as ministry the work that they do in response to their faith. It doesn't matter if this "work"—this ministry—occurs within the life of the Christian community (the liturgy is the work of the people of God) or in the broader community of the world around us. People, ordained and lay, need to identify their actions as ministry when they happen in the name of Christ. In some recent meetings in small rural congregations as part of a shared ministry experiment in Maine, the most common question asked after studying Paul's statement to the Corinthians about the varieties of gifts was, How do I know what my gift is? How does one individual, one believing Christian person, begin to identify the power of God's Holy Spirit working in his or her life? There *is* a variety of ways to work in service to Jesus Christ as we respond to our faith. But how do we begin to articulate the value of these "gifts" and identify these "ministries" for what they really are? It is not enough to believe that the Spirit of God can and does work in the lives of those who believe. People have to identify how and when this happens in their everyday experience.

This is a need, not just of the lay person, but of the ordained person as well. Each of us, regardless of training, skills, or educational background, is called to act on what he or she believes. Each must respond in actions that reach out and serve the needs of others as did Jesus himself. This is the beginning of ministry in the lives of many people: moments when, through faith, they reach out in response to the need of another and know that God has been involved in this action through the power of his Spirit. Critical in our lives as Christians, these moments must be called what they are—the ministries of God's people. These moments of ministry can be shared by each member of the fellowship of faith.

## Actions That Implement Shared Ministry

In order to work effectively—in order to minister—each person in the worshiping community has to discover his or her useful purpose and respond to it. The actions that we are suggesting are specifically related to the lay Christian, but it is obvious that interaction with the ordained person is vital, or many of the suggested actions will not take place. Since the role of authority and leadership in most congregations is assumed by the ordained or commissioned person, his or her involvement in these actions can greatly affect the total outcome of the actions on the life of the congregation.

Three actions are basic: education, encouragement, and support. The first must be a *conscious* effort to reeducate ourselves regarding the meaning of ministry and its application. Few people would argue with our basic definition of *ministry* or find trouble accepting the fact that ministry applies to the lives of all of us. However, in our churches we do not see the working out of what we say we believe ministry to be. Perhaps, one reason for this is that we have learned what ministry is intellectually, but we do not know experientially. For example, a child can be told many times that he must not touch the stove because it is hot. He or she knows intellectually that the stove is hot because other people have said so, but it is not enough to know that the stove is hot as a fact or a piece of information. Eventually, the child must experience the fact that the stove is hot; so he or she puts a finger on it. From that moment on the child truly knows that the stove is hot, not only because he or she has been told, but also because he or she has experienced the fact.

Most people who go to church today are familiar with the word *ministry*, where it comes from and how it is acted out in the life of the Christian community. Intellectually, they know what ministry is. How many know the meaning of ministering because they have done it? Our problem is that we only know what ministry is through intellect and not through experience. For this reason, we need education that incorporates the experience with information. People need to experience the varieties of possible ministries as they respond to their faith in everyday actions.

In the small congregation it is particularly difficult to generate such opportunities. Ministry has traditionally been seen as the function of trained, commissioned persons. If, as in many small congregations, the services of such a person are part-time or sporadic, the initiative and leadership for creating these learning experiences is curtailed. If the person providing leadership and initiative does not see this as part of his or her task (often ministry is perceived only as maintaining services of worship, visiting the sick, and so on), then the opportunity for the average person to take part in leadership will be further reduced. What often happens in a small congregation is that the "ministry" is carried on by the trained person when he or she is there. Meanwhile, the members of the congregation see their "ministry" as raising money. The basic purpose of the church—ministering to the needs of one another and to the community—is overshadowed by the most immediate need for survival.

The ordinary person in most small congregations (perhaps in most congregations regardless of size) lacks the confidence and skill to proclaim his or her share of the total ministry of that congregation. Unless the person with authority provides leadership and learning experiences to build confidence and develop skills, many congregations will depend on the clergyperson to "do the ministry" for them while the members worry about money and property. Further results are a sense of powerlessness in relation to denominational structures (diocese, synod, or the like) and a feeling of failure as a people.

Educational experiences in ministry can and should be many and varied. Some occur in the context of a traditional learning experience such as a study group, Bible class, or church service. Others happen as people interact in less formal meetings which are not organized to accomplish a specific purpose. When someone takes on the responsibility of a Christian education program, a social action program, or any other part of the church's work, there will be opportunities to assume leadership, to build confidence, and to learn ministry. When one person is encouraged to reach out and respond to the need of another because of his or her faith commitment, then the opportunity to practice faith and to learn the meaning of working in the name of God is created.

This type of education is often ignored within our churches. We have become conditioned to value the educational experience that is designed, planned, and coordinated in a definite setting to produce a specific response. Certainly this more formal type of education will always be useful and necessary, but there is more to education than just knowing the facts. We learn through doing and responding with our hearts and souls as well as through our minds. Especially for the Christian, for whom action is an outgrowth of belief, education is never solely intellectual.

Time must be given, as Christian people share their lives in community, to identify these more casual and sporadic educational opportunities. The way we learn and what we learn in daily interaction need to be seen as basic parts of our Christian education. In identifying how this happened in one congregation, a member said, "The difference between St. Mark's and most of the other congregations I know is that the laity at St. Mark's work harder to remember that the basic problems of living provide the opportunity for deepening our Christian experience."[6] In sharing life experiences, whether joyous or not, people learn to minister to one another and to understand ministry.

The second necessity in developing the participation of lay persons is encouragement. In the average congregation there is little encouragement for each believing person to assume the responsibility of doing ministry. "The pastor is the minister, that's his job." "After all, he (or she) has been trained to do these things." "If anyone is sick in the hospital, just call me (the pastor speaking) so I can go visit them." These statements are heard over and over again in churches of all denominations. Is the pastor the only person in the congregation who can minister? Certainly not, but when there are no efforts made to encourage other believing persons to do the job, it will be performed by the clergy alone.

The responsibility for encouraging more active participation is certainly not just that of the ordained person. However, when the clergy are hesitant to encourage lay people in the doing of ministry, lay people hesitate, not wanting to tell the minister how to do the job since he or she is the person trained to do it.

A member of the project committee of a shared ministry experiment in Maine said recently that one of the best things about her minister was his willingness to step back, let other people in the congregation do what needed to be done, and trust their ability to do it. She spoke of an occasion when people in her congregation were encouraged to respond locally to the hunger crisis. A weekly luncheon was organized at which little was eaten, discussion was initiated about the problem, and the money was used for a variety of purposes. Sometime later, her clergyman told of some people in the congregation responding to a family in sickness when he could not be there; in discussing it later, both he and the people involved discovered how much ministering had taken place. There seemed to be a correlation between the clergyman's encouragement and the people's automatic response to another, somewhat different, task of ministry. Once encouraged to do something they had not done before, and satisfied that they had done the job well, they responded to another situation and ministered spontaneously.

Ordained persons must let go of the reins they hold so tightly on the work of the Christian community. They must encourage others to share that work without imposing their own fears and demands. They must be willing to trust that each person who believes *will* respond out of his or her faith commitment through the power of the Holy Spirit. When the clergy take this initiative (which is a sign of their own faith commitment), lay people will feel a freedom to respond.

The third area of action, which builds on the first two, is support. People can learn through experience and act on what they know to be true, but they also need the support of those around them to strengthen their conviction to believe and act continuously as new opportunities arise. This kind of action is equally important in the life of the ordained person; a pastor too needs to feel support in his or her ministry.

In the Episcopal church in Maine, one of the most important aspects of the life of the clergy in recent years has been the clergy support groups, set up by the bishop, which meet on a regular basis for mutual support, encouragement, and sharing of common tasks. At a recent clergy conference on the enablement of ministry in the same diocese, there was discussion of the clergy supporting lay people in their ministries as they have felt supported themselves. Now that they have experienced the value of support in their lives and ministries, they see the need of supporting the ministries of lay people in their congregations. One clergyman said, "I'm beginning to see how little I have supported people in the things I have asked them to do. Usually, I have only complained when they haven't done it."

We recently visited several small congregations in the extremities of Maine. On a two-day visit to an area the size of Rhode Island (it has three churches served by one pastor), we met with a group of people representing the three congregations and with the pastor to explore the meaning of shared ministry in their situation. The response to the meeting was more than we expected on a Friday night, but even more impressive than the size of the group was the enthusiasm with which both the pastor and the lay people talked about each other's work and the support each gave the other. The pastor openly acknowledged the cooperation, willingness, and actions of many people in each congregation which allowed him to function over such a broad terrain. The people said with basic simplicity that they were able to do so because the pastor trusted, helped, and encouraged them to do necessary and important things. It was evident that these Christian people, ordained and not ordained, could reach out in a caring spirit with a sense of purpose, hope, and joy because they felt the support of one another in the ministry that was theirs together.

Support can be provided in many different ways: through a group and through personal encounter; through sharing similar frustrations or listening carefully to someone's individual struggles; when people need our concern and when we need theirs. However it is given, two things are clear: (1) Within the context of the Christian experience, each person (clergy and lay alike) needs the support of others; and (2) people can learn to support one another if they care enough. One observation from a congregation in which people have struggled to share the ministry helps sum up the matter: "Every congregation can learn the basic troubles of living together if it has the right support and guidance. Congregations that never learn the first lessons cannot go on to the more difficult lessons of evangelism and mission."[7] The support extended within the Christian community is critical to the doing of ministry and the living out of the church's mission.

This chapter has dealt with some basic issues relevant to sharing ministry within the church, both through exploring the meaning of the word *ministry* and suggesting some actions that can initiate stronger participation of lay persons in the total ministry of any congregation. It is our firm conviction that, within the congregational setting, people can learn to live together, act on their faith, and minister to one another. The ministry that comes from this witnessing community is the work of God in us through the power of the Spirit for which each member of the community shares the responsibility. As Hendrik Kraemer stated lucidly almost two decades ago in *A Theology of the Laity*:

> The good news is that God, source, end and Lord of the created world, is by His own divine initiative active to restore things to their true nature, and invites men to enter into this stream of divine liberation. The whole membership of the Church is by the fact of its membership through baptism in principle within the stream of the invited.[8]

## NOTES

1. John Knox, "The Ministry in the Primitive Church," *The Ministry in Historical Perspectives*, ed. H. Richard Niebuhr and Daniel D. Williams (New York: Harper and Brothers, 1956), p. 1.

2. Urban T. Holmes, III, *The Future Shape of Ministry* (New York: Seabury Press, 1971), p. 3.

3. Ibid.

4. Task Force on Ministry to the Small Church to the 113th General Assembly of the Presbyterian Church in the United States, *Strengthening the Small Church for Its Mission*, Appendix B.

5. James R. Adams and Celia A. Hahn, *Learning to Share the Ministry* (Washington: The Alban Institute, 1975), p. 3.

6. Ibid., p. 61.

7. Ibid.

8. Hendrik Kraemer, *A Theology of the Laity* (Philadelphia: Westminster Press, 1958), p. 93.

# 7

# Programming in Small Congregations: Factors Which Aid or Limit

*Jeffery S. Atwater*

This chapter describes factors which tend to aid or limit programming in small congregations, gives examples of programs actually being used, and offers suggestions for programming in some congregations. It does *not* attempt to propose a full, complete, ideal program from outside any particular congregation.

My primary frame of reference is New England church life in small towns where my ministry is set. Small congregations in more urban settings may or may not exhibit the qualities described here, but it is likely that some of what I suggest is applicable in various settings. I draw on twelve years experience as a pastor of small churches in Vermont, New Hampshire, and upstate New York, contrasted with three years as one of four ministers on the staff of a twenty-four-hundred-member Congregational church in Detroit, Michigan, and one year as one of three ministers of a twelve-hundred-member church in Topeka, Kansas, while I was a fellow in pastoral care and counseling at the Menninger Foundation. Since 1970, I have been pastor of the

Lyme Town Ministry, a yoking of the Lyme Congregational Church (United Church of Christ) in Lyme, New Hampshire, and the First Baptist Church (American Baptist) in Lyme Center, New Hampshire.[1]

## Factors Which Aid Programming in Small Congregations

### Less Frantic Pace (*"You mean the phone doesn't ring every five minutes?"*)

Life in small congregations, particularly in small towns, moves at a slower pace than it does in larger congregations. There tends to be a little less pressure to do a myriad of things. It is possible to concentrate resources and energies on fewer projects.

Yet people in small congregations can become harried as a fast-paced style of living invades their domain via television and other media, including denominational mailings constantly suggesting expansion of programming to include yet another "emphasis" or vital ministry. Still, relatively speaking, folk in small congregations are often under less pressure than their more highly programmed, large-church counterparts.

### Opportunity to Be Personal (*"Sure I have time. Come on in."*)

A slower pace permits a more personal ministry. Fewer members means the pastors and the lay leaders in a small congregation can personally know and relate to a greater proportion of the membership than may be possible in a larger church. Programs can be designed to meet the *known* needs of people.

### Church's Sense of Identity (*"We're a community church."*)

Small congregations sometimes have a clearer sense of their identity than do large ones. Often this image of themselves is expressed with pride as a kind of watchword: "We are a community church and want our church building to be used by people and groups in town whether or not they are members of this church." Or, "We are a church which can support its own minister, and we do not have to yoke with another church."

There are strengths and weaknesses in each of these statements. The church's sense of identity can get in the way of good programming, but where it is in line with the mission of Christ in that community, this commonly acknowledged identity is a strength.

### A More-Stable Population (*Newcomer: "You lived here all your life?" Oldtimer: "Not yet!"*)

Many small congregations are in communities whose population is relatively stable. Members may have lived there most of their lives except for service in the armed forces. Stable populations allow for long-term relationships and continuity in programming often not possible in communities where people move in and out frequently.

The disadvantage of stable populations is that decision-making power tends to settle into the hands of a few oldtimers. With relatively few people moving into these communities bringing fresh ideas and new enthusiasm, church programming can stagnate.

### Opportunity for Close Professional Relationships (*"Hello, Bill? This is Jeff. Say, about Mr. Jones . . ."*)

Small congregations, especially in small-town or small-city areas, can establish close relationships with professionals in various human services agencies. There are fewer agencies, and each is smaller than in a higher population area. A pastor can know personally the doctors his or her parishioners see, the nurses and social workers in the hospitals, the welfare workers who serve the parish area, and the local police and judges. Many of these persons can become resources for valuable preventive programs in the church and community, as well as professional colleagues of the pastor, enabling him or her to minister intelligently.

## Factors Which Limit Programming in Small Congregations

### Limited Income ( *"You can't get blood from a rock!"* )

Many small congregations suffer from inadequate funding. They are often located in relatively poor areas economically. Small towns often have lower pay scales than urban communities and limited options for employment. Commuting to distant jobs is increasingly expensive. Most small-town people have relatively modest incomes and have never known anything else. Their financial expectations for themselves, and for their church and its pastor, tend to be low. Money is given in relatively small amounts, often as a single yearly gift or when the person happens to attend church. There is still resistance to pledging.

People in small communities are frequently reluctant to engage in a full every-member canvass. Rugged individualism still prevails. People are unwilling to ask their neighbors for money, even for a good cause such as the church. They use printed stewardship resources sparingly and often reluctantly, for to them it reeks of Madison Avenue and is foreign to their image of themselves and of their neighbors.

With money scarce to begin with, and a reluctance to go after what is available, many small congregations realize inadequate income.

### Inadequate Building ( *"How do you heat this barn?"* )

Many small congregations are saddled with a beautiful (or ugly!) historic building which is far from functional for today's needs. Huge "auditoriums" are seldom even half-filled with worshipers. Church school teachers struggle valiantly to be creative and make attractive learning centers in corners of high-ceilinged rooms which seem designed by the devil himself to bounce sound around. Meanwhile, the cost of utilities continues to skyrocket, gouging ever-larger chunks out of the church's total income.

### Poorly Budgeted Programs (*"We haven't any money to rent a film."*)

Workers in small congregations may recall times when a good program was about to be tried until it was discovered there was no money in the budget. Small congregations sometimes have to use nearly all their income to maintain a pastor and the building —often not doing justice to either—and programming suffers.

### Short-Term Pastorates (*"He's a nice young man, but he'll only be here two or three years. I know, I've seen them come and go."*)

Small congregations can be plagued by an unending series of short pastorates. Three years is often the maximum time a pastor can stay before he or she must move on for pressing financial or professional reasons or because it takes one faction that long to heat things up enough to make further fruitful ministry impossible.

### Lack of Long-range Planning (*"Lent? But it's only November!"*)

Short pastorates are one reason small congregations fail to do much long-range planning. It is difficult for either the pastor or the laypersons to invest energy in making plans likely to be interrupted by a change of ministers.

Limited finances also dampen enthusiasm for long-range ventures.

**Low Expectations** (*"I never thought of that."*)

Programming in small congregations can be limited by lack of awareness of what is desirable and possible. People may be quite satisfied with what is happening and not press either the pastor or themselves to try anything new.

There is also a kind of hand-to-mouth attitude which operates in many small congregations. "Getting by," rather than expending precious human energy or more of the church's limited income, may be the hidden motive behind program decisions.

**Resistance to Change** (*"We never did it that way before."*)

Small congregations, particularly in small towns or rural areas, are notorious for being resistant to change. They tend to be conservative and to have limited experience. They may be oldtimers or the younger generation of established families who are pillars of the church and have a vested position to defend. The desire to be a big fish even if in a small pond has led some to throw their weight around, usually on the side of keeping things safely within familiar bounds where they exercise control and have status.

**Few Leaders** (*"Who would like to be chairman? [silence]"*)

Lack of sufficient leaders is a weakness in many small congregations. There are not many people to choose from, and more jobs than leaders. Additional programs are difficult to launch when existing ones are taxing the leadership energies of the few to the breaking point. Leaders in small churches are frequently leaders in several other community organizations, including local government. "Fatigue-of-the-faithful-few" is a real factor to contend with in attempting to improve the programming of the small congregation.

### Few Followers (*"I'm not sure I can make it."*)

Even if a small congregation comes up with a good "chief" for a particular program, there may not be enough "Indians" to go on the expedition. The best laid plans do not amount to anything if nobody participates.

### A Defeatist Attitude (*"We can't do it. We're only a small church."*)

Most small congregations have had enough "failures" to be leary of great expectations and to get tired of trying. They fail to sustain good programs or initiate new ones because they feel the response does not justify the effort.

One penalty of living in a small community for a long time is that cynicism develops as one gets to know people all too well. Becoming accustomed to their lack of interest over a period of time, one can "write them off" and cease to invite them to participate in new programs when, in fact, the time might now be right for a positive response.

### Old Grudges (*"I'd rather fight than switch!"*)

Another human frailty shows up clearly in congregations in which there are not enough people to hide it or nullify its effect. Personal animosities have a way of disrupting things and lingering to poison the life of a small church; the damage they inflict can be out of proportion to the differences among members. If only the energy expended to nurse old hurts or to counterattack could be harnessed for the cause of Christ, programs could really come to life and bring life.

### Suggestions Concerning Programming in Small Congregations

**Take Time** (*Wise conference minister to new young pastor: "Give the people time to get to know you and trust you."*)

This is good counsel for a new pastor approaching programming in a small congregation. Beware of trying to do too much too soon. Getting a locomotive all steamed up and opening the throttle does not move a freight train. You have to be sure the cars are on the same track and connected to each other and to the engine.

**Be Personal** (*"You bet I'll be over, Jim."*)

Take advantage of the slower pace often found in smaller communities. When people appreciate a life-style which allows time for visiting, it makes sense to value informality and provide ample opportunities for it. Perhaps cathedrallike solemnity is not altogether possible as people gather for worship in a small congregation. Some pastors may need to rethink the theology of worship they learned in seminary when confronted with the obvious joy and warmth people in a small congregation express as they greet one another in church on Sunday mornings.

Personal contact with many parishioners is possible at their places of work in the communities. Local stores, gas stations, lunch counters, banks, and the post office are places where the pastor can bring the church's ministry to people personally.

Pastoral calling is not a lost art in small congregations. Where it is possible, desired, and expected by the people, the pastor has the expectations of the community to reinforce his own inclination to call on people in their homes. This old-fashioned practice is still one of the best ways of getting to know people in their real-life situations. Personal knowledge allows the pastor and lay leaders to plan programs which are relevant to real needs in the parish. It also makes it possible to involve people in the program-building process where their personal interest and talents fit.

One difficulty with carrying out a good program of pastoral calling is that small congregations, like their larger sisters, have many families in which both adults work outside the home during the day. This need not mean that effective pastoral calling is impossible. Joseph McCabe[2] has given excellent counsel on calling on families systematically by appointment.

In small congregations pastoral calling can be a vehicle of communication and a builder of community spirit. One rural Vermont pastor spoke of his function as being almost that of a town crier. As he made his rounds in the more isolated parish homes, he discovered how hungry people were for news of other folks in town. Without becoming a gossip, he was able to be a message-bearer on the human level as well as in the vertical dimension of bringing the gospel to people.

This same pastor spoke of growing awareness that he had to articulate explicitly the religious or spiritual dimension of his calls lest he simply "visit" about the weather and local news. On his calls he now encourages singing hymns around a piano, if there is one in the home, reads Scripture, and often offers a prayer. His testimony is that this makes his home calls both humanly refreshing and spiritually worthwhile. Personal sharing and bringing news is a feature which is still possible and valuable in the small rural congregation.

A great attraction of the small congregation for some pastors is the opportunity for an intimate and personal ministry to a greater proportion of members than is possible in a large congregation. Small churches allow for more one-to-one ministry because the pastor is not forced to use as much time and energy administering a large, complex, and multifaceted program. However, lest one become naively romantic about small congregations, one must remember that large churches have the advantage of additional staff persons (such as assistant pastor, full-time custodians, and

secretaries) who do much of the work that some pastors of small
congregations do out of ignorance, choice, or necessity. Cranking
the mimeograph or replacing altar candles can use up time which
was theoretically free for personal ministry.

Programs in small congregations are likely to be related to
people's needs because the group is small enough for people to
know one another rather well. Good programs truly meeting the
real needs of people are not impersonal. Nor are they an obstacle
to good pastoral relations. They are the vehicle by which an
effective pastoral ministry can be carried out. There cannot help
but be a difference between relating to five people and to fifty
people in any given span of time. Take advantage of the size and
be personal.

### Provide Needed Services (*"There's a new you coming every day."*)

Do what is relevant. Do not waste energy trying to do what
does not fit your situation. Be good stewards of resources, both
financial and personnel, but be willing to venture and try new
programs too. All this presupposes that the leadership, both
clergy and lay, has taken the time to know and be known personally by the wider parish community they serve.

Learn people's needs. Provide *needed* services. Enlist people to
help meet one another's needs. The elderly can telephone other
older or shut-in members daily. This provides a checkup on both
and gives them a feeling of being needed and useful, which they
truly are.

As a pastor and people of a small congregation know their
community intimately, they can spot the gaps in services and can
focus the church's ministry accordingly. For example, in the
Upper Connecticut River Valley there is a need for housing for
older persons who are no longer able to maintain their homes
because of increased property taxes or declining health. Representatives from several churches in the area have been working

for over a year to build a comprehensive retirement community where people from surrounding towns and rural areas could live in a familiar country setting, with easy access to needed services.

A minister in North Conway, New Hampshire, has developed a whole church community building of services not otherwise provided for people in that community and a wide surrounding rural area. His philosophy has been to see a need, mobilize resources to meet it, and, once a program is established, encourage it to become independent. In this way the church can move on to reinvest its resources in a new program to meet another need.

### Expand People's Horizons (*"Wow! I never knew that before!"*)

One factor limiting good programming in small congregations is the low expectations of the people. Often they simply do not know of anything better. A perennial opportunity of congregations in small communities is to plan programs which will expand the experiences of the local people. Youth-group exchange meetings with larger churches in metropolitan areas have been arranged for years, but what about something similar for adults?

One of the values of statewide denominational annual meetings and ongoing committee work is the widening of horizons which occurs as people travel from home to mingle with folks from other communities and churches. Good ideas as well as good fellowship are shared. People usually discover some good things about their own local churches in addition to learning ways to improve programs.

This sharing can also occur in a local area. The New Hampshire Conference of the United Church of Christ is experimenting with a program called Parish Partners in which a layperson from one church becomes actively involved part-time in the life of another church. He or she may attend worship occasionally, observe and perhaps participate in some of its board and committee meetings, and come to other programs or special events. Gradually, as trust develops, the parish partner becomes a two-way communication link, sharing good ideas, tried-and-true programs, and resources with both churches. A vital part of this program is area-wide meetings of parish partners to compare notes and debrief one another on their experiences. The circle of sharing widens, and learnings are reinforced as they are "taught" to others.

### Be Flexible (*"Maybe that is the best way after all."*)

Small congregations have many things in common, but they also have differences. Each parish is in some respects unique. The leadership needs to take this into account, particularly pastoral leadership, which comes into the community from the outside when the new pastor arrives. Flexibility in adjusting to the particular parish is essential. Without abdicating his or her leadership role, the pastor of a small congregation will do well to be teachable. Pet programs which worked well in other parishes may be suggested but seldom insisted upon in the early years of a pastorate. Several years of living together as pastor and people may be needed before each really understands and accepts the wisdom of the other's ways.

I am pastor of two small churches located three miles apart in the same town. One is reasonably well organized with the usual boards and committees which operate "normally," that is, according to my expectations, which are based on what I learned in seminary and experienced in other parishes. The other has few boards or committees and no regular schedule for their meetings. Whatever needs doing, people tend to let go until someone finally gets on the phone and obtains others' approval to do it. After five years of frustration and skepticism I have been converted. Their way probably works as well in their situation as "the right way." Be flexible.

**Use Seasons of the Year** (*"Don't miss our annual [you name it]."*)

Small congregations in northern New England are blessed with four distinct seasons, and they use them well in program plans. Strawberry festivals, ham-and-baked-bean dinners, sugar-on-snow parties, hunters' breakfasts, and wild game dinners are examples of events geared directly to the seasons. Small congregations already use the seasons well with these established traditions, but there may be additional opportunities.

One innovative pastor in Wells River, Vermont, created an "Apple Sunday" during the autumn harvest of 1974. He gave an apple to each worshiper and then used apples throughout the service to illustrate biblical truths. The people were delighted and have insisted that this become an annual event.

**Use the Church Year** (*"Every time I come to church they're singing either 'Silent Night' or 'Christ the Lord Is Risen Today!'"*)

Making use of the church year is another way small congregations can have good programming. Educating people into the rhythm of life and the drama of salvation by using the church calendar is valid in any size congregation. Advent workshops to make gifts for others, Christmas caroling to shutins, Christmas Eve candlelight services from which each worshiper takes the light of Christ back to the home, Lenten study groups, Maundy Thursday communion services with the ancient rite of Tenebrae, ecumenical Easter sunrise services, offerings like the One Great Hour of Sharing and World-Wide Communion Sunday, all help provide a framework for one's pilgrimage through another year of life.

A personal ministry directly tied to the church year is the practice of bringing the sacrament of communion to shutins on the Sundays when it is served in church. A deacon or other lay reader accompanying the pastor on these calls can be an added blessing to those called upon. It also provides a time of fellowship and leadership training for the pastor and deacon. I learned anew the value of touch and human caring when I saw an older deacon lean over and plant a kiss on the cheek of the town's eldest citizen, a lady in her nineties, after bringing communion to her. To see her beam and to ponder how long it might have been since someone showed her such warm affection has led me to a deeper appreciation of the value of touch and has altered my style of ministry significantly. "Leadership training" can go both ways.

### Have Celebrations (*"Kites for Christ? In church?"*)

Many small congregations are apologetic about their buildings and discouraged about their program limitations. Stoic resignation is often more apparent than Christian joy.

In recent years, perhaps because of dissatisfaction with pressurized routines which entrap many people, there has been in our culture as well as in the churches a new emphasis on special celebrations to act out our happiness and joy or, perhaps equally, to entice us into feeling happiness and joy. Whatever the reasons, people are becoming more openly demonstrative in churches, even in small congregations.

A pastor in Lebanon, New Hampshire, added verve to the annual September Rally Day Sunday by actually flying a kite from a fishing pole in the sanctuary during worship. After a noontime church family dinner he led the congregation in a kite-flying celebration on the town common. Such events may not be appealing or appropriate in all situations, but they emphasize the potential for childlike joy. Every congregation, no matter how tiny, has things worth celebrating. Build celebrations into the program.

## Use People's Talents (*"I just know you are the one who can do it."*)

Small congregations tend to overwork the faithful few. A perennial search for new leadership needs to be carried on even though it may occasionally bump up against the wishes of vested interests. Gentle ways of easing people into responsibility need to be found rather than catapulting them from obscurity into the limelight of a make-or-break situation.

Small congregations in communities where the population is relatively stable may suffer from a lack of new people to involve in the life of the church. When new people do show up, they are often either ignored or desperately latched onto as blessed relief for tired troops. A common example is the immediate recruiting of new members to teach church school because they mention they have done it before. One fine point of church leadership is learning to respond appropriately to the presence of newcomers, neither ignoring them nor frightening them away by quickly asking too much.

Discovering and encouraging the use of people's talents is an art. Church leaders can become so involved in planning and administering programs that they do not have time to know members as persons. Yet this is exactly what is necessary if they are to call forth talents in the service of Christ.

A wise and experienced pastor of a Vermont village which includes a good proportion of highly educated and sophisticated residents who have retired there from responsible positions all over the world says he must constantly guard against planning more and more programs which would consume ever-increasing amounts of his time and energy. Rather, he chooses to seek out and utilize the talents of others and encourage them to do their own thing. This attracts additional persons to participation. The church's program is announced in a weekly newsletter which he writes in a delightfully folksy style and yet with a deep and explicitly theological content. There is a strong emphasis on the arts, including musical programs of exceptionally high caliber, films by a nationally known creative film-maker, and a theater group of some fifty local people. These "Parish Players" now perform light and serious drama all during the year in churches, homes, gas stations (yes!), and colleges throughout northern New England. His counsel is: "Programs are not to fill time, but must be for the purpose of making a difference in people's lives." These are words of wisdom for any church, small or large.

### Work Cooperatively (*"You mean we don't have to compete?"*)

Small congregations tend to be isolationist; so do many pastors. Both pastors and lay leaders are learning that that can make a very lonely and limiting combination and that there is joy in sharing.

I can testify to the change in my ministerial style which has come about through participation in clergy colleague groups. Such groups bring six to ten clergy together for a three-day initial conference followed by at least six months of colleague meetings. Self-selected topics of professional practice are considered; members take turns presenting. Working out of each person's strengths becomes a lesson in valuing oneself; having one's weaknesses accepted by others serves as a lesson in self-acceptance. The variety of individual talents and program ideas which members of the group share with one another is an inspiration. Trust grows quickly; instead of hiding our lights under a bushel, they are shared so that all may benefit. Various combinations of group members are now working together on specific programs for their churches. Programs are being enriched as talents of "outside" ministers are brought in without fear or jealousy. Programs too ambitious for one congregation alone are now becoming a reality and blessing several churches at once. Recently an overnight prayer retreat brought out thirty persons from four churches and their surrounding communities. There was the added joy for each participant of meeting new people and getting out of the rut of always being with the same few persons from one's own small congregation. Work cooperatively. It improves programs, and it is fun!

## Use Imagination (*"How about . . . ?" "Yes, that might be fantastic!"*)

Small congregations need to make use of their particular situations. There are opportunities all around for creative and exciting programs which will touch people's lives helpfully. "Lord, give us eyes to see!"

One small town has an annual "Pumpkin Festival" started by a church school teacher (my wife) who thought the town needed something different which would be fun for kids but also involve adults. A Saturday morning in October saw children bringing pumpkins they had grown to the town common for a "contest." There were enough categories to assure that each child would win a prize given by local merchants. The event was fun for everyone. The next spring, pumpkin seeds were given to every child in school with instructions to ask older residents in town for advice on growing giant pumpkins. This fostered sharing between the generations and between "old natives" and "young newcomers" in town. The event has now grown to include a Halloween costume parade; the firemen bring out the firetrucks to escort the little marchers, a farmer gives pony-cart rides, and everybody visits with neighbors.

Another "seed project" grew out of a Lenten adult discussion group following Sunday worship. A young high-school teacher wanted his church to do something for all people of the community. He suggested that members go to each house in town, give the people a small gift, and invite them to come to worship on Easter Sunday. Someone suggested that the gift be a packet of seeds symbolic of new life. The local hardware store owner agreed to order them. Another person designed and mimeographed a simple folder with a drawing of flowers on the cover. After worship on Palm Sunday, over a dozen adults and children worked side by side coloring in the flowers on the covers and stapling packets of seeds inside next to the message which read: "We want to share these seeds with you in hopes that we, as a community, may grow together. Won't you join us in church on Easter Sunday, or attend the church of your choice?" A brief poem and the schedule of Easter services completed the pages. These folders were delivered to virtually every home in the community (over four hundred). People were surprised and pleased; much goodwill was generated for the church—all because one person identified a need, and people shared their ideas, used their imaginations, encouraged one another, enlisted help, worked together, and did something for someone else.

That is not a bad model for church programming.

### Conclusion

Many factors which affect programming in small congregations are beyond the immediate control of the church—geography, climate, overall economic conditions, and basic human nature. However, two factors over which the church should be able to exercise control are inadequate income and short pastorates. These persistently frustrate small congregations.

Short pastorates are the norm for many small congregations. A church that frequently experiences the loss of its minister is repeatedly in grief and mourning. This grieving uses emotional energy which might be available for the church's program of service to its community. It is poor emotional and financial stewardship to allow the pattern of short pastorates to continue unabated.

Two things obviously are needed. One is significant stewardship education issuing in real commitment so that the church is adequately funded. Most small congregations desperately need increased income to support their pastors and to allow for more comprehensive programming. If it is truly not possible to secure this income locally (and this is seldom the case), then some forms of denominational (or ecumenical) support must be devised.

The other need is for both clergy and laypersons to place a higher value on the small congregation and to overcome the apologetic and defeatist attitude, which, in true American style, equates smallness with inadequacy. We need real commitment to the small congregation as a valuable place where God dwells and through which he works out his purposes.

After all, God must love small congregations, for he made so many of them. Programming in small congregations will improve when we believe that small can be beautiful!

## NOTES

1. In addition to drawing on personal experience, I have had the counsel of fellow pastors in the Grafton-Orange Association of the United Church of Christ and in other neighboring churches. I am deeply grateful to Judith Peterson Atwater and the Revs. Adrien Arschliman, Eunice Bull, Mason Ellison, Norman Dubie, Sr., William Geertz, Peter Gilbert, Richard Manwell, John Marsh, Alan McCain, Bradford Rehm, Robert Robb, Thomas Roden, William Ruhl, and Edward Tyler.

2. Joseph E. McCabe, *The Power of God in a Parish Program* (Philadelphia: Westminster Press, 1959) pp. 13–20; and *How to Find Time for Better Preaching and Better Pastoring* (Philadelphia: Westminster Press, 1973) pp. 9–18, 33–47.

# 8

# Resources of People, Money, and Facilities for the Small Congregation

## *Robert L. Wilson*

The local congregation is a social institution requiring a minimum of resources in order to fulfill its purpose. This chapter will deal with three resources—people, money, and facilities. It can be argued that the basic resource is people because they provide the money that pays for building, hires pastors, and purchases goods and services.

I will focus on the church of small membership and limited resources. The very existence of such a congregation may be threatened by the lack of a sufficient number of people to provide a minimal level of program and leadership.

Churches with membership of less than two hundred persons are likely to have resources insufficient or barely adequate to maintain the institution and carry on a program.

The adequacy of resources for the operation of the small church is determined by two factors. The first is the number of members and their level of affluence or poverty. A small congregation of wealthy individuals can employ a full-time pastor, erect a church building, and maintain a range of activities. A group of similar size made up of persons with modest incomes would not have adequate funds to do so.

While the amount of resources available for a given congregation is finite, a basic article of faith of denominational leaders is that people can and should give more to the church than they do. The goal is always to raise more money for the work of the Kingdom, however that is defined. Given the reluctance of people to part with a portion of their possessions, this assumption seems to be well founded.

A second factor which determines the adequacy of resources is the expectations of church leaders and members for the local church. Resources are adequate if they enable the institition to perform in the manner which the participants consider proper and effective. Expectations will vary among churches of different denominations and to some degree among churches within the same denomination.

Expectations change over a period of time. What was considered an adequate church program twenty-five or fifty years ago is not acceptable today.

## Changing Church Standards

The concept of an adequate church has been changing as part of a general trend in society toward demanding a greater variety of goods and services. The consumer today has a broad range of products from which to choose; a variety of services are available to the individual although they are not necessarily convenient or satisfying. Anyone who has attempted to deal with a big impersonal bureaucracy or to travel by train can provide ample illustrations.

The expectations for the church have followed the trend to a more varied and complex local organization. The congregation is expected to be large enough to subdivide into age groups (children, youth, young adults, adults, senior citizens, and so on) and interest groups (missions, social action, Bible study, choir, bowling teams, and so on). To maintain such a variety of activities requires a group of skilled leaders, both volunteer and professional. It is not uncommon to hear denominational leaders refer to a "full church program." This simply means the variety of activities which are the accepted standard and are possible only in the church with a large membership.

The changing expectations of acceptable congregational style can be noted in the deployment of clergy. The trend has been for congregations to press for the exclusive services of a pastor. In general, ministers also prefer to serve only one congregation. A result in some areas and denominations is that more pastors are serving fewer churches.

This phenomenon is particularly evident in the United Methodist Church in North Carolina, a state which has a large number of small rural congregations. In 1950, there were 1,879 churches served by 772 pastors or 2.4 churches for every minister. In 1974, the state had a total of 2,056 United Methodist congregations served by 1,214 ministers, and the ratio of churches to clergy was 1.7. In the twenty-four-year period the number of congregations increased 9.4 percent, but the number of pastors serving them grew by 57.3 percent. During the same period the total lay membership increased 22.5 percent. The expectation that each congregation should have its own pastor has been implemented by many churches with the result that more ministers are serving fewer congregations and fewer lay people.

Apart from the general trend in society toward higher expectations, what forces determine the acceptable norm for the local church? The standard is to a large degree set by the professional leaders including the clergy and denominational administrators and staffs of specialized boards and agencies. Rank-and-file church members usually are not aware of the latest theological trends or the newest educational theories and methodologies. Appropriate professionals in the denomination are employed to bring these to their attention.

Church structure is designed by professionals. How the denomination and the local church are to be organized is determined by the clergy and denominational leaders. When the parent body either requires or urges that each congregation have certain organizations (that is, a committee on missions, a committee on Christian social concerns, and so on), it sets a standard for church style and program and assumes that resources will be available.

Desired norms are conveyed to members of the congregation through church periodicals, church school literature, and programs which come from denominational agencies. Probably the most effective communicator of the appropriate congregational style and program is the local pastor. He or she interprets the denominational expectations and has the responsibility of securing the resources necessary to attain them.

The professionals in an organization tend to push for a greater level of activity, the latest and most sophisticated methodologies and more rigorous standards. They have been educated to do so. The higher educational requirements for ministers were not adopted as a result of a demand by lay people but by the clergy themselves. The Doctor of Ministry degree, which has achieved some popularity recently, was brought into existence by professionals (clergy who wanted to upgrade their skills and status and theological schools which needed a new product to keep their staffs gainfully employed). There has been no general outcry by lay people in the congregations for their pastors to secure this additional training.

## The Expectation of Ineffectiveness

As Arthur Tennies noted above, the image of the successful church that has been communicated to the small congregation is one that it cannot replicate. There simply are not enough potential members to enable the church to have the range of age groupings, staff, and facilities considered necessary.

The result is that many small congregations develop a kind of inferiority complex. Because they have neither the people nor the funds to carry on the activities which a church is supposed to maintain, they may see their congregations as ineffective. Defeatism and apathy can prevent the small church from realizing its potential.

This raises a fundamental issue of the relationship of the Christian gospel to the social institutions which exist to promulgate it. Is an effective Christian witness limited to a certain form of social institution? The answer obviously must be no. Ample historical evidence is available to demonstrate that the Christian message can be proclaimed in a multitude of forms.

By setting a certain institutional style as normative, the denomination implies that churches which cannot conform are less than adequate. By institutional criteria, (number of members, size of budget, variety of program activities, and so on) some congregations will inevitably be judged less than adequate. A result can be a kind of self-fulfilling prophecy. By defining themselves as inadequate, small churches may assure that they are.

## Resources Available to Small Churches

### People

No church is ever satisfied that it has the maximum number of members. One congregation decided that when it reached fifteen hundred it would recruit no more members but direct persons to other churches of the denomination. As the membership approached fifteen hundred, the ceiling was raised to two thousand.

The small church too feels that an influx of members would be desirable. In point of fact, many small congregations will not grow significantly. If they are going to continue to exist, they must do so with fewer members than the denominational leaders consider to be the optimum.

While the small church cannot be strong in numbers, it does possess some unique strengths. The members have a sense of ownership about the church and its program. They know they are needed. Indeed, everyone must bear a share of the responsibilities if the congregation is to function. This is the reason a higher proportion of the members of a small church will be found in attendance than in a large church; they know their presence is essential and that they are missed when absent. One cannot hide in the small church as in the large.

People are inclined to support institutions over which they have some degree of control. The probability of becoming an official in a congregation of one hundred is much greater than in a congregation of one thousand. People will have greater loyalty to institutions they help direct.

The small church provides fellowship and support. (A similar situation may exist within a subgroup of a large congregation such as a Sunday school class; the emphasis on the small group, interestingly enough, began in large churches.) It enables the individual to feel part of the total group. Intergenerational relationships are part of the life of a small church; they must be structured in large ones. These factors contribute to the intense loyalty many members have to the small church.

The major resource of the small congregation is not numbers, but the loyalty and devotion of the members and the time and energy they are willing to give to its maintenance and ministry.

## Money

A matter which consumes much time and energy in churches of all sizes is money. For the small congregation the issue may be one of life and death.

Every congregation must meet certain financial obligations if it is to continue. A pastor has to be paid, a building maintained, utility bills met, and various supplies purchased. When a congregation's financial base is marginal, all the people's energy may go into keeping the institution alive. There is danger that survival may become the congregation's sole purpose.

The membership necessary to provide an adequate financial base will vary with the affluence of the congregation, their concept of an appropriate contribution, and the program desired. It is not uncommon for a mainline denomination to close a small church only to have it come back to life as an independent congregation with a part-time free-lance pastor. In such a case the people elect to have a "cheaper" church. As an independent congregation they have no denominational overhead or mission program to support. The part-time pastor earns his living in some other job; so there is no required minimum salary. In these instances, program is reduced to fit available resources.

The members' concept of adequate stewardship and the pastor's expectations will determine the number of members needed to support the church. I talked with the pastor of a small, extremely conservative congregation that had sixty-eight members and supported a full-time pastor. A comment was made about the probable financial problems of such a small group. The pastor replied, "Yes, money has been a problem; we need five more families to put the church on a firm financial footing."

One problem is that there may not be sufficient funds to meet the rising expectations of both congregation and clergy. The people may desire the services of a full-time minister and not wish to share his or her services with other churches. The denomination has set a minimum salary. The pastor expects certain facilities and program materials to be available. The disparity between expectations and income is a major source of tension in the small congregation.

Another problem for the small church is regular outside subsidy, usually in the form of funds to supplement the pastor's salary and usually from the denomination. Subsidy is a problem because it creates a kind of institutional dependency. The local group may relax and depend on denominational funds to balance the budget. The people may resent the agency from which they receive subsidy because it is a symbol of their dependency and the agency staff may wonder why the local people do not show initiative. Furthermore, since subsidy programs depend on mission funds from larger congregations, they are always subject to being redirected to other programs which may catch the attention of the denominational leaders. A long-term subsidy can be fatal to a congregation. A vital voluntary institution must be self-supporting. In regard to subsidies for local churches, it is indeed "more blessed to give than to receive."

A concern often voiced is that a disproportionate part of the income of a small church must be used to pay the minister's salary. This is of course correct. It is not uncommon for a congregation to put 40 to 70 percent of its income into pastoral support. For such churches the pastor is the major resource, the essential ingredient for the church to be able to continue its program. That a major portion of the church budget is required for the support of the minister is not a negative factor.

Some complaints about the proportion of funds going into the pastor's salary come from denominational staff and agencies whose support comes from the benevolent contributions of the congregations. Because they are supported by what are in effect local church surplus funds, that is, money not absolutely necessary for local expenses, they have a vested interest in seeing that such funds are available. Christian people should contribute to causes outside their local church and community; however, the basic unit of ministry is the congregation. Church boards and agencies exist to be an extension of or to provide services to the local churches, not the other way around.

Money will probably always be a problem for the small church, but if it is to have any sense of independence and integrity, it must over the long term be self-supporting. It may do this in a variety of ways (that is, sharing a pastor, being part of a larger parish, and so on). What is important is not the method, but the result.

### Facilities

Many small rural churches own obsolete structures erected in an era when preaching services were the main activity and several Sunday school classes were held simultaneously in different parts of the sanctuary and the church basement. Such church buildings lack the kind of space which can be used for a range of program activities. The one-room church with fixed pews, while adequate for preaching and worship and acceptable for some Sunday school functions, cannot be used for a variety of other congregational activities.

While the buildings occupied by small congregations leave much to be desired, they have one major asset: They are located in virtually every community in the country. Thus the church has a physical presence in society; it is located where the people live and it is accessible.

A major problem is the feeling of many small congregations that they are unable to update or replace their facilities. They may fail to secure appropriate expert help when building or remodeling and thus make inadequate use of their resources.

Small congregations can have adequate facilities, and many do find the resources to provide them. An example is the Rural Church Program of the Duke Endowment. This private foundation makes grants to North Carolina rural Methodist churches for buildings. It requires that an architect be employed to design the building and pays one-half of the fee. Additionally, grants are made to the church to assist in repaying its building debt. The timing of the grants is related to the amount of debt outstanding, providing an incentive for early repayment. The total amount given to a local church will range between 5 and 20 percent of the building cost.

There are two significant results of this program. First, small churches get the best building for their investment, and the structures are designed for maximum flexibility and usefulness. Second, the congregation saves thousands of dollars in interest by paying the mortgage ahead of schedule in order to qualify for the final grant. It is not uncommon for a ten-year loan to be paid in three to five years. While there is an outside incentive to encourage the congregation to secure expert help and to raise funds quickly, the program illustrates what resources lie dormant in some small-membership churches. The evidence is that small churches have more resources with which to provide adequate facilities than may be generally realized.

## Management of Resources

Limitations on the resources available to the small church can be offset to some degree by more efficient use of what the congregation already has. Churches of all sizes frequently fail to make the best possible use of people, money, and facilities. Good stewardship would dictate that every effort be made to use these resources with maximum effectiveness and efficiency.

Churches do not manage their resources well because they fail to determine clearly their goals and the means of reaching them. A congregation may drift from year to year, repeating activities simply because they were done in the past. A vast amount of time, energy, and money may be spent on programs which only marginally contribute to the central purposes of the church. Because priorities are not set, important items may receive minimal attention while peripheral activities consume much time and energy.

There are three areas in which churches manage resources poorly. The first is the use of lay persons' time and energy. People are urged, even pressured, to participate in meetings for which there often has not been adequate preparation, which last too long, and which accomplish little. Activities which merely fill time are sometimes given a sacred aura because they are related to the church. A result is that the church does not have the resources to carry on its major reason for existing.

A second resource which is not always utilized efficiently is the pastor. The trend has been for more pastors to serve fewer persons. It might be assumed that because the minister had fewer members (and thus fewer pastoral calls, hospital visits, and so on) he or she would have time to engage the nonchurched portion of the population and church membership would increase. Denominational statistics do not indicate that this is happening. Apparently more lay members must be getting more, if not necessarily better, pastoral service. While pastors tend to be busy, their time and energy are diffused over a multitude of tasks, some of which could adequately be done by volunteers or possibly left undone. Like some congregations, the minister's work may lack clear and attainable goals. The pastor is a valuable and expensive resource which should be managed efficiently.

A third resource which is not always used efficiently is the church building. The major reason for inefficiency here is that structures are erected without adequate flexibility for a range of programs. Buildings are designed to house certain kinds of activities. When different programs are desired, the church building may not be adaptable.

A small church may or may not have expertise within the membership to deal with building needs. Because of the perceived limitation of funds, such a congregation may be reluctant to employ an architect to design and supervise new and remodeled buildings. The result too often is that the church does spend less on a building project, but it pays dearly over the long term because it has a structure which is inadequate for the church program and unadaptable when changes are desired.

## Purpose and Method

The theological definition of the church and the goals for which it strives are based on criteria other than size of the congregation. The witnessing and supportive Christian community can be any number of people. The witness and ministry is carried out by a social institution, but the values which the church exists to promulgate are not determined by that institution.

Every congregation, whatever its size, needs to develop a clear definition of purpose, including the responses that the church desires from individuals and a definition of a Christian life-style, both within and outside the congregation.

While the small-membership church can fulfill the theological goals of the church, it may be unable to meet the cultural expectations. The small-membership congregation may be found quite inadequate in organizational terms. It may not have enough people to fill the offices required or suggested by the parent denomination. There may not be sufficient members to subdivide the congregation into age groups or enough tenors for a really good choir. While this will, of course, limit the activities of a church, it does not limit the transmission of the gospel. To hold that viewpoint would be to say that the methodology is more important than the message, a position that would be unacceptable for Christians.

For the church leader with a rigid concept of an essential church program, the congregation with a small membership is a stumbling block. The individual who is convinced that there must be a church school class to parallel each grade in the public school will find the small church frustrating because it can never live up to that expectation.

In the administrative area the small-membership church fails to satisfy many church leaders. In fact, the major problems of such churches are not theological but administrative, and they are both acute and continuing.

The first aspect of the administrative problem is that the small-membership church cannot meet the expectations of the pastor. It does not have the people, money, or facilities to carry on the program that the minister has been taught is normative. Even more important, the small congregation may not have a sufficient financial base to pay the pastor an adequate salary. The denominational administrator sometimes has a difficult problem finding clergy who will accept an appointment to or a call from such a congregation. This situation has traditionally been met by congregations sharing the services of a pastor. While this has had the advantage of securing a salary which enables the several churches to employ a minister, often the expectations of each congregation cannot be met. There is, for example, only one eleven o'clock hour on Sunday each week; therefore, only one of the churches that share a pastor can have a service at that time every week.

Denominations have attempted to solve the administrative problem of the small church in two ways. The first has been by means of subsidies which assist such churches to pay their pastor's salary. I have called attention above to several problems that subsidies raise. A second method of supplying professional leadership for small congregations has been to organize them into parishes of various kinds. This has usually involved two or more pastors or other professionals serving a large group of small congregations. Such attempts have usually originated with the denominational leaders and have lasted as long as there was adequate outside subsidy or a particularly congenial group of pastors on the scene. They often have not been able to survive over the long term or through a change of ministers (see chap. 9 for a fuller discussion of this issue—ED.).

The basic question for the small-membership church is theological: What is its nature and purpose? From this comes a second question: How may the resources of people, money, and facilities be used most effectively to achieve this purpose? The nature and purpose of the church is the point at which one begins to develop the institution and utilize the available resources to achieve the desired objectives.

# 9

# Organizational Structures for the Small Congregation

*Alan K. Waltz*

In considering organizational structures for the local church, most denominations are caught in a dilemma. On the one hand, a denomination seeks to provide an organizational style or system that is workable in each local church. On the other hand, it is concerned about providing a distinctive character to the total organization and to interrelate the various levels in the denomination. In most cases, denominations have not been able to solve this dilemma because polity stresses one goal to the detriment of the other.

The development of a churchwide polity has been an essential aspect in the corporate life of a denomination. It has been rather generally assumed that all parts of the denomination should be governed, not only under the same doctrinal statements and major policy statements, but also under the same well-defined, specific polity statements and structures. Problems have arisen, especially in large and diverse denominations, because a single model of polity and organizational structure has not fit many local stituations.

Two assumptions have influenced much development of local church polity. First, church-wide legislative bodies have seen virtue in a single approach to local church structure and governance. They have given primary attention to developing an organizational scheme which could be transmitted to local congregations. They provided organizational models which encouraged standardized boards, committees, activity patterns, vocabularies, and reporting systems. The advantages to the top and middle judicatory levels are obvious: Only a single system needs to be promoted, resourced, and tabulated for performance.

The second assumption relates to what is perceived as the typical church. Generally, the average local congregation is assumed to be larger than it actually is. It is assumed to have between five hundred and seven hundred members; in fact the average church is in the range of two hundred to three hundred members. In part, this is because those on national legislative bodies come from larger congregations and legislate out of their experience. Partly, it is due to the desire to deal with the administrative and structural problems confronting the larger churches that are seen as more complex, difficult, and important.

How does one find appropriate structures for small-membership congregations? In recent years a new awareness has arisen concerning their pervasiveness in the denominations. This is not to say that a majority of the membership of the denominations is in these churches, but these are the units for which organization and structure are legislated. Again, renewed awareness has shown that the small-membership congregation is found in all settings—large cities, small cities. rural towns, and open country. The uniqueness of the organizational and structural needs for the small-membership congregation results, not from its geographic location, but from its size.

This chapter considers some concepts related to small-membership congregations and relates them to organizational concepts in the hope that they will provide some tools with which to search for new possibilities for small congregations.

## The Starting Point

The starting point for a discussion of organizational structures for the local church must be its needs and perspectives. Various legislative bodies should make organizational proposals for the local units. The requirements of the total denomination and/or its general agencies are rather well perceived and are often imposed on local churches. What is not well understood are the requirements and capabilities of the local church. To provide an adequate, viable organizational scheme for small-membership congregations, one must have a clear understanding of their unique qualities, characteristics, and possibilities.

A report of a study of the church in rural Missouri summarized one set of findings as follows:

> For denominations with centralized authority, the small rural church presents a special problem for the denominational levels. The denomination has a program of activities and a model of congregational organization that the small church may not be able to fulfill, at least not to the denomination's standard. Thus, the small rural congregation appears inadequate. Attempts are being made to bring local congregations into the mainstream of denominational activity through consolidation or cooperative plans such as the "larger parish" or "group ministries."[1]

The starting point for most in the denominational hierarchy, including senior executives, regional executives, general agencies, resource persons, and, in many cases, ministers, is the perspective of the denomination as a whole. The only group consistently removed from this perspective is the laypersons in the local church. The generalization is that the smaller the local church, the less likely are the members to share the denominational perspective.

Inhibitions are placed on a congregation by the polity and structure developed at regional and national levels. Prescribed procedures limit options, impose restraints, indicate form and direction, and carry a generalized assumption of the ways in which congregational life should be organized and operated. In some cases, especially for small-membership congregations, these rubrics are too demanding and restrictive, and they mitigate against successful organizational patterns and styles. Requirements from external sources can divert energies and resources to activities that are not important or relevant for the local church and can make the congregation feel inadequate to the point of only partially attempting the procedures or opting out entirely.

However, general procedures and structures should not be considered only as negative factors, for there are numerous advantages to an overall polity, including the development of common procedures, terms, and resources which can be utilized throughout the denomination. Further, shared organizational models develop corporate understanding and identity. Congregations and ministers can be stimulated to participate in activities in which they might not otherwise become involved. Centrally developed procedures can serve as important conceptual frameworks for the local congregation.

A delicate balance must be maintained. If one imposes a system or controls it too tightly, creativity and interest are stifled, especially in the smaller units. The need is constantly to keep in mind the middle ground between external control and local autonomy so that participants will be actively involved and interested in their immediate situation and in the larger denominational units. The denomination has the right to offer information and organizational models, but it does not have the right (or should not fully utilize it if it does) to impose them.

How can you help people become involved in doing what they do well? This is the key question. One can organize people only around their interests and needs. As the concerns and priorities of local church members are understood, one finds ways in which to organize the necessary tasks.

The argument here is not whether polity and organizational

statements should be developed at the denominational level, but that the focus must be the local church, whatever its size. Organizational models must recognize the uniqueness and the integrity of the local church. The starting point must be with the local congregations; regional and national organizational structures must adapt to local needs.

## The Nature of the Small-Membership Congregation

Much difficulty in developing viable organizational patterns arises because we have no clear understanding of the nature of the small congregation. A congregation is a unique group of persons with its own integrity, history, customs, and traditions. It has developed shared experiences and expectations over a period of time. Unfortunately, this integrity or uniqueness is often overridden in order to satisfy requirements of regional or national bodies. The small-membership congregation is often treated as an immature child; no recognition is given to its ability to plan for itself and make decisions. It should be considered as a unique, whole, mature unit with its own character and personality. We should consider it as we would any individual, as being of inherent worth, notwithstanding whatever status we may ascribe because of attributes related to size.

By definition, the small congregation has a limited number of participants. The working definition relates to the number of persons in the membership or active fellowship as contrasted with congregations with substantially more participants. Certain corollaries follow. The smaller congregation has fewer persons available for leadership positions, fewer resources upon which to draw, and fewer programmatic requirements. This in no sense implies that it is inferior but simply that it has a different character.

A small congregation is not necessarily unviable or close to extinction. Indeed, some of the strengths desired in large churches are found in small congregations, and these unique characteristics have helped the small church to survive, as research on churches in rural Missouri indicates.

As local churches become more dependent on denominational centers for program, organizational models and leadership (clergy), they are more subject to influences of these same centers. Our most general conclusion is that rural churches have to some degree avoided the dependency relationship and therefore are not highly sensitive to centralized influences. . . .

A finding was that sect-type groups in aggregate had a better survival record than church-type groups. By definition sect-type groups were not as involved in the activities of the larger society, and the sect-type concept suggests the establishment of moral communities based on immediate membership. This idea can be extended to denominations within the church-type organizational set. Those less structured (e.g., Southern Baptist) showed better survival experience than the more structured (e.g., Methodist and Presbyterian).

The characteristics of local congregations' programs may insulate them from the influences of the larger society. Programs tended to be turned inward emphasizing worship services. . . . The ubiquitous Sunday school is another evidence of the self-maintaining characteristic of the church program. Sunday schools can be a completely laymen's activity. . . . Resistance to complex organizations are also apparent in the lack of official boards in many churches and the irregularity of their meetings in still more.

The fact of low financial support for rural churches is also a statement of low financial obligations. The simple building and minimum expenses for professional leaders exempt the rural churches to a large degree from economic constraints. . . . If aspirations are for an elaborate program, then many rural churches are too small, but if the rural church is perceived as a fellowship group, then a congregation might exist "where only a few are gathered together."[2]

The small congregation may be different not only in size but also in kind. The larger society and the denomination as a whole tend to assume that the experiences of the large and complex structures pervade all parts of the system. This in fact is not the case.

The differentiation can be made in the concepts of the primary and secondary group. Larger congregations reflect the characteristics of secondary or impersonal groups. In many instances the small-membership church still adheres closely to what Charles H. Cooley termed the *primary group* concept.

> By primary groups I mean those characterized by intimate face-to-face associations and cooperation. They are primary in several senses but chiefly in that they are fundamental in forming the social nature and ideals of the individual. . . . Perhaps the simplest way of describing this wholeness is by saying that it is a "we." It involves the sort of sympathy and mutual identification for which "we" is the natural expression. . . .
>
> Primary groups are primary in the sense that they give the individual his earliest and most complete experience of social unity and also in the sense that they do not change in the same degree as more elaborate relations, but form a comparatively permanent source out of which the latter are ever springing.[3]

The evidence from the extensive study of the churches in rural Missouri points to this characteristic in small churches.

> In reformulating our conception of congregations of rural churches we finally regard the congregations as primary groups. In this respect, the neighborhood schools and the rural church, although having much in common, have taken sharply divergent paths. The neighborhood school has been incorporated into the complex educational system finding standards, resources and control at the state and national levels. From neighborhood institutions, schools have become specialized groups which are removed from direct community control through professionalization of staff, standards of curriculum, and extra-local evaluation. At the same time, consolidation of schools through state requirements has effectively eliminated the open country schools and changed the locational patterns of other primary and secondary education units. . . .
>
> The rural church . . . has not followed the same course. It has remained neighborhood and community dependent and oriented. Specialization, in the form of organizational elaboration or leader-

ship roles, has been minimal. The moral precepts of the church are likely to reflect those of the community and the different local congregations can accommodate the particularism on which primary group relations are maintained. In addition, as other groups such as the school become more secondary, the primary group quality of the rural church may take on added importance. In general, the study of the rural church informs us of the dynamics of rural society and suggests an addendum to a monolithic influence on urbanized social systems in the local community.[4]

If we are convinced that the small-membership church has unique characteristics and qualities, this should reflect in the organization and structures developed to support these congregations. They should preserve the sense of individual worth, integrity, and uniqueness of any congregation, including the small-membership congregation. One should also recognize the relative strengths and weaknesses inherent in the small congregation and take into account the character of the interaction in the smaller fellowship.

## The Primary Activities for Which Organization Is Required

An examination of the life and work of the local congregation and of congregations on the basis of size makes it apparent that small congregations have limited programmatic and organizational needs for which to plan and organize.

Worship services and Sunday school are almost universal activities for the small church. Even when the preaching service is not scheduled weekly, church school activities are often held each Sunday. The small church has adapted to providing these activities on a minimal or subsistence basis. Lay leadership is strong and active. The costs of professional leadership are kept low by sharing a pastor with other congregations, by using less well-trained ministers, or by having lay preachers whose primary income is from a secular vocation.

Many church studies have indicated that only a limited number of other activities are likely to be found such as a women's organization, a youth organization, a choir, and some type of administrative board. Small congregations concentrate on worship and educational activities and relate to their fellowship experiences. They are not disposed toward internal committees or task forces and are not often oriented to secular activities and causes. They remain relatively self-contained and removed from the ebb and flow both of society and of the denominational unit.

The small congregation has no need or desire for a large and involved organization structure. Many have established means for doing the necessary administrative work. They have few requirements in terms of the development, maintenance, and administration of facilities. The church plant is limited in size and simple in nature. Trustees, as part of their active participation, often care for and maintain the property.

The requirements for professional leadership are also minimal as compared to large congregations. Often, the minister is nonresident. Linking or yoking congregations makes it possible to share ministers and parsonages.

The primary group nature of the congregation means that programmatic and organizational activities are cared for informally as the need arises. The formal structures imposed externally, especially required report forms, are often hindrances or nuisances to the organizational work within the parish. As authors of one study put it:

> It is hazardous to predict the future of the rural church but its tenacity in a changing society suggests that another survey in a decade would find the bulk of the congregations operating at the same stand and at about the same level of activity. They will continue to be essentially fellowship groups engaged in internal activities and a frustration for denominational executives.[5]

## Intracongregational Structural Options

In light of the preceding, let us consider some organizational options for the small church which recognize its unique character and still allow for meaningful interaction with larger denominational units.

The first option is a single group which meets as needed to care for the necessary business of program and organization. Such a group can be described as an administrative board with broad powers. It can link the congregation with the regional and national denominational structures. Those items essential to the denomination can be cared for in this setting. The description of this unit should be as short as possible and should allow the local group as broad a range of behavior as possible. It would recognize the strengths inherent in the local congregation and yet would assist the congregation to interact with the denomination as a whole. Its goal would be to provide structure, without unduly restricting or imposing outside character, for the informal, face-to-face meeting of concerned persons, emphasizing the accomplishment of tasks within the context of the fellowship.

If the congregation's size requires a more complex structure, some major subdivisions of the key administrative unit can be made along functional lines. For most smaller congregations, these would have to do with educational activities. Relationships between these groups should be rather loose or relaxed; the primary goal in the division of labor is to see that activities are performed for the good of the total group. The precise nature of the organization is less important than insuring that the needs of the congregation are met in a manner that is acceptable to the members.

Care should be taken to judge the amount of structure a small group can support. Many denominational models for the local congregation, if followed to the letter, would require between sixty and seventy-five persons if no offices were held by more than one person. For churches with memberships of less than one hundred, this is patently absurd, and for those with between one hundred and two hundred members, it is at best difficult. Such a requirement forces the local church to ignore (in the face of official criticism) much of the formal pattern and establish leadership positions and organizations on paper only, thus compromising the integrity of the group, or else to refuse to comply. To levy requirements which cannot be met is foolish at best and demeaning at worst. The balance between the large organizational system and the needs and character of a small fellowship should be sought.

Both parties will be best served by negotiation of a style to which both the individual congregation and the larger system can accommodate. The specifics of the organizational model are less important than the manner in which agreement is reached.

Reporting procedures should be sufficiently flexible to allow congregations to report on work accomplished rather than on organizational models served. Reporting methods are usually developed to serve the larger organizational needs and perspectives. Instead, they should be developed to reflect progress, initiative, and activity in functional areas and to serve the needs of the local unit. This can be done without sacrificing the desired comparability throughout a region or a total denomination, but it will require a reorientation of all concerned to the task and rationale of organizational reporting.

In summary, internal structures for organizations need to facilitate the work of that unit. In the case of small congregations, structure should take into account their character as unique, small, primary social groups with a sense of purpose, both for their own activity and for their joint activity with other congregations in the denomination. Organizational systems designed primarily to serve the needs of the denomination or of middle-sized to large churches will not find ready acceptance in the small congregation. It would be far better and less frustrating to all to examine first the needs of the congregation and then all the other desired ends.

## Extracongregational Structural Options

The individual congregation can be linked organizationally to others in a number of ways. These range from linkages which flow up and down the organizational structures of a denomination to cooperative and ecumenical ventures with other congregations in the community. Or the congregation can elect to remain autonomous from other communions and indeed from any association or denominational ties.

Small churches particularly have related to different forms of cooperative ministries or parishes. In part, this stems from the individual congregation's inability to provide a "full range of program" or attract qualified ministerial leadership. Partially, it reflects the desire of regional and denominational officials to provide viable organizational settings for program and for the support of the professional clergy.

Many people have summarized the types of organizational models for joint activity. Marvin T. Judy, in two books, *The Cooperative Parish in Nonmetropolitan Areas* (Abingdon, 1967) and *The Parish Development Process* (Abingdon, 1973) has done a good job of this. These forms can be briefly summarized as follows:

*A station or single church.* As the name implies, the church functions as a single entity with one or more pastors.

*Circuit.* Two or more churches are served by a minister. It generally occurs among churches in the same denomination whose financial resources are linked to provide salary for a minister. The congregations are organizationally separate.

*Consolidated church.* Two or more churches join together to form a single congregation. This involves the complete merger of the former bodies into a new unit.

*Federated church.* Two or more churches from different denominations combine to form one congregation while retaining their individual denominational identities.

*Yoked field.* A circuit composed of two or more churches from different denominations served by the same pastor or staff.

*Cluster.* A number of churches in a geographical area grouped together for specific purposes which may be specific or diverse. In some instances, clustering serves administrative needs; in other instances it is designed to further programmatic concerns.

*Enlarged charge.* A circuit of two or more churches in which many activities are undertaken on a charge-wide basis rather than on an individual basis. Activities include the governing board, educational tasks, trustee functions, and the like.

*Extended ministry.* A large and relatively strong congregation shares its ministry and resources with another congregation, usually smaller and less self-sufficient.

*Group ministry.* Within a geographical area, a group of churches join together in a voluntary association to enhance their ministries. A number of ministers may be involved, each having primary responsibility for his or her own church or charge. However, under the terms of the agreement forming the group ministry, certain skills, resources, and activities are shared.

*Larger parish.* A group of churches are placed in a single administrative structure such as a charge conference served by several ministers or professional persons. The churches work together to establish tasks for the total parish and the utilization of resources and staff.

Other organizational forms could be mentioned, but they would essentially be variations on these forms. The structures range from relatively simple ones requiring little interaction with other congregations to large, complex associations of congregations requiring precise rules for governance.

The important issue is that the organizational form carefully take into account the needs of individual congregations. The voluntary nature of these relationships is important. Often administrative forms are imposed upon congregations by denominational officials seeking to serve the organizational needs of other parts of the system.

In the United Methodist Church, bishops and district superintendents have the power to appoint ministers to local churches. Often they seek to establish situations which will provide adequate salaries for the ministers. They have the authority to link churches to form pastoral charges into circuits. Unfortunately, in many instances, the primary motivation has been to satisfy the financial needs of appointed ministers, and not of the churches involved.

In most denominations in the 1960s there was an active attempt to "deal with the small-membership church" by promoting the organizational schemes listed above. Often a key motivation was to reduce the number of "marginal" and "inefficient" units and to simplify the administrative and programmatic tasks of the denomination.

In considering any organizational structure or style which would link congregations, attention must be given to the integrity and worth of the individual congregation. The values in the small congregation need to be preserved and enhanced in the larger arrangement. Of course, the advantages in such an arrangement should also be thoroughly explored.

Often, participation in a larger organizational unit imposes on the small congregation a range of activities which is burdensome and indeed foreign. The values of the fellowship association may be lost to the presumed good of enhanced programmed activities and professional leadership. The individual congregation should exercise its own rights of decision making and self-determination.

In a time which stresses helping the individual move to full personhood, with all the risks that entails, we must also encourage local churches, whatever their size, within the broad limits of denominational polity, to come to full "personhood" in the determination of organizational linkages. Indeed, we must also be prepared to deal with the congregation which elects to remain isolated or even to die.

## Developing Viability

The perspective advocated here may seem utopian. I have described a different approach to the administrative and organizational activity of congregations. The key to organizational structures is not the particular form or style but the recognition of the uniqueness of each group and its needs.

Through the 1960s, two countervailing trends occurred in the church. Ministers were encouraged to become "enablers" and "enhancers" of the skills of lay persons at the same time that organizational structures were becoming more centralized and demanding. Part of the thrust of recent convolutions in the major denominations has been the redistribution of decision-making powers. Local congregations, especially those considered less than self-supporting or "full-range" churches, have been asked to work in organizational settings not of their making, to their liking, or suitable to their needs.

Karl Deutsch, in an article "Toward a Cybernetic Model of Man and Society," reflects upon the increasing complexity of society and the relative freedom and rigidity of structures. He speaks of the concept of complementarity or the mutual enhancement of various, similar, and dissimilar parts of a structure to function for the common good.

The degree of complementarity between the members of a society may determine its capacity for sustained coherence, while their degree of freedom—and their range or readjustments available without loss of complementarity—may determine the society's capacity for sustained growth. If the essence of growth, according to

Toynbee, is increase in self-determination, then this concept of growth should prove applicable to societies and other complex learning nets. The more complex and readjustable the constituent parts of a society become, the greater the coherence and freedom of each of its subassemblies, the greater should be the society's possibilities of itself achieving greater coherence and freedom in the course of its history. Learning nets and societies do not grow best by simplifying or rigidly subordinating their parts or members, but rather with the complexity and freedom of these members, so long as they succeed in maintaining or increasing mutual communication.[6]

We have leaned toward subordinating the needs of the local congregation to the requirements of the total body, imposing an all-encompassing system which has refuted the concept of integrity and worth on the local level and stifled whatever local initiative and promise there might be.

To accomplish the common good we may need to rely not so much on a common structure as upon common and shared information about purpose, intent, and direction. Those informed and motivated can generally find the organizational model appropriate to the corporate task. The preoccupation with organizational models comes about because of inability or unwillingness to articulate and disseminate concepts of organizational purpose and goal.

In *Small Is Beautiful*, E. F. Schumacher explores the values of thinking in terms of small economic issues and working in a limited area with limited resources to accomplish the goal of productive, meaningful employment. He pleads that an economy of small production units can fulfill the common good of society, and he stresses the need for adequate communication. In the following passage Schumacher addresses this issue which is relevant to our discussion in the context of organizing many units, such as local congregations, for a combined function. To coordinate diverse small units in the accomplishment of the common task, Schumacher sees four functions as necessary.

The function of communications—to enable each field worker or group of field workers to know what other work is going on in the geographical or "functional" territory in which they are engaged, so as to facilitate the direct exchange of information.

The function of information brokerage—to assemble on a systematic basis and to disseminate relevant information on appropriate technologies for developing countries. . . . Here the essence of the matter is not to hold all the information in one centre but to hold "information on information" or "know-how on know-how."

The function of "feedback," that is to say, the transmission of technical problems from the field workers in developing countries to those places in the advanced countries where suitable facilities for their solutions exist.

The function of creating and coordinating "sub-structures," that is to say, action-groups and verification centers in the developing countries themselves.[7]

If we replace the term *countries* with *local churches*, a model begins to present itself. The structure within each unit or between units is not nearly as important as the interconnection of concern and information.

The problems in most denominations occur not because of inappropriate and irrelevant organizational structures, although this is a contributing factor, but because the denominations have not established their precise purpose in the contemporary world. As a result, they have been unable to communicate to their constituent parts the information necessary to challenge, obtain the interest, and direct the energies of all their units. The small church has been peculiarly influenced by this problem because, as the denomination focuses on organizational requirements, it develops systems in such size and detail that small congregations can not meet the full range of requirements and expectations. The inadequate flow of information as to purpose and direction then sets up a condition in which frustrations develop on all sides and become mutually reinforcing.

Viability in all congregations, especially small ones, depends on recognition of the fundamental integrity and worth of each, regardless of its external characteristics. Viability comes with awareness throughout the entire denominational system of the bonds which unite. Viability comes as there is shared understanding of the total task and direction of the denomination and of the role each unit can play in terms of its location, resources, history, leadership, and skills. If there is a shared sense of the combined task and the role each can play, the organizational structure is essentially unimportant. With little shared sense of the common task, the larger system may seek to impose commonality and unity through structures, reports, and vocabulary. The more these are imposed, the greater will be the resistance to full participation. Viability comes not from size or resources, but from a recognition of the unique role and contribution which can be made to the total organization.

## Summary

The small congregation is not a peculiar and isolated phenomenon but the modal unit in every denomination. It has strengths and weaknesses. The tendency in the immediate past has been for denominations to develop strategies and structures which have not been realistic for small congregations. The latter have been placed in a position of being unwilling or grudging participants in an organizational scheme.

Redress of this situation lies, not in new structural models and ingenuous techniques, but in developing an understanding and appreciation for the integrity and worth of each congregation and then relating each to the overall concerns of the denomination. The local church must be recognized as a small intimate fellowship with need for a limited range of structures and activities.

The precise nature of internal structures is less important than the development of an environment in which fellowship groupings can function without artificial and stifling organizational restraints. External structures and relationships with other churches are important only insofar as they recognize the inherent worth of the congregation as it interacts. The small congregation can bring strengths to cooperative ventures of all types, provided these strengths are recognized and preserved.

The congregation becomes a viable part of the whole to the extent that it shares the hopes and dreams of the total body. It cannot be forced to accept a point of view by structure or polity. It can be actively enlisted to the work of the whole through the sharing of information, through the concern of the parts of the system for one another, through the mutual enhancement of the ministry of each part, and through the shared expectations and purposes of the total. If these things are done first, specific structural models and styles can be of help; if they are not, organizational structures become repressive at worst and ignored or freely adapted at best. As with individuals, recognizing the inherent worth of the unit, sharing the common task, and allowing for freedom and creativity are primary considerations which must underlie organizational structures for small-membership congregations.

## NOTES

1. Edward W. Hassinger, Kenneth J. Benson, James H. Dorsett, and John S. Holik, *The Church in Rural Missouri 1967.* Research Bulletin 984 (December 1971) University of Missouri-Columbia, College of Agriculture, Agricultural Experiment Station, Columbia, Missouri, p. 26.

2. Edward W. Hassinger, et al. *A Comparison of Rural Churches and Ministers in Missouri Over a 15 Year Period.* Research Bulletin 999 (November 1973) University of Missouri-Columbia, College of Agriculture, Agricultural Experiment Station, Columbia, Missouri, pp. 23–24.

3. Charles H. Cooley, *Social Organization* (Glencoe, Ill. Free Press, 1956), pp. 23, 27.

4. Hassinger, et al. Research Bulletin 999, pp. 24–25.

5. Hassinger, et al. Research Bulletin 984, p. 27.

6. Karl W. Deutsch, "Toward a Cybernetic Model of Man and Society," *Modern Systems Research for the Behavioral Scientist,* ed. Walter Buckley (Chicago: Aldine Publishers, 1968), p. 399.

7. E. F. Schumacher, *Small Is Beautiful* (New York: Harper & Row, 1973), pp. 202–3.

# 10

# New Expectations: Denominational Collaboration with Small Churches

*Theodore H. Erickson*

Many small maken a great.
CHAUCER

"The Little Brown Church in the Vale" is a nostalgic reminder of the impact that tiny communities of faith have had on the development of persons. "The Small-Church Problem" is an institutional concern symptomatic of an age when size and growth are considered vital signs of life. While both perspectives permeate the attitudes of church leaders today, neither is adequate. We need new concepts which are both descriptive and normative, definitions which enable us to describe the current situation and to posit realistic goals.

The term *small church* immediately raises a question: Small in relation to what? Several methods of description can be used. One is statistical. For example, the mean membership of all United Church of Christ churches (members divided by churches) is approximately three hundred. However, because of the small number of disproportionately large churches and the large number of disproportionately small churches, the average size is in reality closer to one hundred eighty members. Second, a small church can be defined as one in which the number of active members and the total annual budget is inadequate relative to organizational needs and expenses. It is a church struggling to pay its minister, heat its building, and find enough people to assume leadership responsibilities. A third method is in terms of typical cultural expectations. During the past century, churches have been expected to grow, ministers have expected to advance their careers in ever larger congregations, budgets have been expected to increase. Yet by the late 1960s, the high percentage of people who professed church membership and the population cohort ratios resulting from the low birthrate in the 1940s made church growth generally problematic.[1] The large number of ministers seeking positions in a small number of sizable congregations made career advancement impossible for many, and inflation had begun to eat away the increased per capita giving. A psychology of failure began to run rampant through the success-oriented mainline denominations. Small became a feeling as well as a fact.

Growing churches usually exhibit a combination of four positive factors: favorable demographic location; professional leadership style and expertise appropriate to the population; a variety of programs to meet a variety of social needs; and a compelling theological perspective. Most small churches are located in areas no longer suitable for church growth. A generalized liberal theological stance is not as widely compelling as it was two decades ago. Appropriate leadership and program characteristics depend on specific, local conditions and needs although there is evidence of widespread member dissatisfaction in both regards. To focus our attention solely on a strategy for membership growth would not appear promising.

In all probability, the majority of United Church of Christ

churches, as well as other mainline Protestant denominations, will remain quantitatively small in the foreseeable future. While some types of churches are growing, most United Church of Christ churches have not experienced significant growth in the past decade. Many churches have remained virtually the same size for a century or more; others have lost members at an unprecedented rate.

The fact remains that small-church members and leaders express the need for denominational assistance and respond positively to programs of intervention. Moreover, the general problems of mainline churches today are not confined to those which are small. Small membership may exacerbate some problems (leadership, finances), but it may be a condition of strength in meeting other problems (flexibility, degree of community). A focus on the small church, therefore, is not simply a focus on the majority of churches; it is a way of addressing the whole question of institutional change.

## Church As Organic Association

The organizational character of the contemporary voluntary church has been described in many ways. For our purposes, I will characterize American churches as "organic associations." In its starkest form, the voluntary association is a combination of individuals who join together to reach either mutually compatible personal ends or some agreed-upon collective ends. Its theory, derived from the eighteenth-century liberal tradition, presupposes a series of rational choices regarding ends and means by each of its participants. As a positive aspect of the state's guarantee of individual liberty, an association is at its best a major engine of social change and a primary source of interpersonal community. Organic institutions, on the other hand, exhibit the characteristics of traditional, established, and generally unquestioned functional relationships with and within the culture. Their strength has been stability in the face of change, and they adapt intuitively to new conditions. As "organic associations," our churches are hybrids. Their organic nature is derived from social class, ethnicity, history (including an inherited theology), and the places they occupy in the culture. Their associational nature is derived from the limited liability they claim among their participants and the typically democratic character of their decision-making procedures.

When both organic and associational factors are strong, size is not as critical as it is when they weaken. The situation among mainline churches in America today, and particularly the smaller ones, can be related to weakened organic and associational factors. Indeed, churches respond to their situations in contradictory ways. In terms of their organic nature, churches protect their cultural places by conserving traditional values and increasing internal coherence. The positive way of stating this tendency operationally is to call for "greater member commitment"; the negative way of stating it is by referring to the "survival syndrome." The organic response necessarily delimits the range of rational discussion as to appropriate ends and means among its members and discourages voluntary exit and entrance based on open individual choices. The disaffected are "dropped from the rolls." Potential members are asked to become a "part of our fellowship." People who favor the organic nature of the church project solutions based on values of faith commitment and reassertion of traditional forms in the face of social change.

Those who favor the associational nature of the church project solutions based on rationally renegotiated contracts espousing new needs and goals in the face of traditional ties and cultural values. In either case, the result is likely to be smaller churches, but with size justified on principle rather than suffered at the hands of impersonal forces.

A church as an organic association has its own integrity, shaped by its biblical, historical, and cultural roots, as well as by the changing needs and aspirations of its members and potential members. Change takes place from within that integrity and cannot simply be willed or managed under a new set of operational procedures. A church that loses a vital relationship with its environment in an effort to maintain a sense of historic integrity, or a church that loses its integrity in a frenetic effort to adapt to new conditions, cannot successfully engage in the necessary process of transformation from generation to generation. Organic questions cannot be resolved with mechanical answers; the level of commitment cannot be raised apart from rational decision making about ends and means.

### Three Fundamental Goals for Small Churches

From this perspective I posit three fundamental goals for small churches: (1) greater institutional viability; (2) greater interpersonal fellowship; and (3) greater community stature.

*Institutional viability* refers to the conditions of organizational life which are necessary for the endurance of any voluntary association. Two sets of factors are essential, one in relation to the needs and aspirations of people in the area in which the church functions, another in relation to the members of the church.

In order to deal with and incorporate the needs and aspirations of people in a given area, a church must first have at its center a core of people who are of the area and are committed to joining with one another around their faith. That core must be related in an intersubjective or deeply personal network, not only of church members, but also of people in the wider community. Through the intersubjective network the church maintains relevance with the specific needs and aspirations of potential members. Such objective relationships as house-to-house calling and advertisements or tracts depend upon intersubjective relationships. Often a church remains small in a growing area because the network extending from the core of the church to the community has been broken. A vital intersubjective network will allow the church to organize its program and worship around the explicit or intuited expectations of a wide spectrum of people. A church relates to the changing needs and aspirations of others through its committed members, its theological orientation, and its programs and worship. A significant gap between church practice and community orientation will reduce the long-term viability of the congregation. Finally, the church must project an explicit identification of that faith, an articulated perspective that symbolizes the ties of the association with the Christian tradition. Church names, denominational labels, or statements of faith convey theological perspectives that communicate more or less meaning to various community residents.

Viability factors include the adequacy of organizational and decision-making patterns, facilities to carry out programs, and finances. The tradition of a free-standing, limited-purpose building supported by voluntary contributions, long associated with a predominantly middle-class norm of free-standing, single-family homes, is increasingly problematic. The cost of maintaining such structures is becoming prohibitive; the social meaning of such structures in a secular, pluralistic, multiple-family-dwelling society is drastically changed; the functions for which such structures have traditionally been designed are undergoing rapid modification. While multiple-use, community-oriented structures have been proposed and in some cases constructed, little work has been carried out with small churches regarding structural alternatives. Denominational initiative is necessary for achieving new designs for old structures and new patterns of financing.

Two viability factors are fundamental in both sets of relationships. Leaders who can give concentrated attention to all these elements are essential. A viable church is one whose leaders continually provide direction, initiate or moderate changes, and interpret new possibilities. A second factor is the ability to enter freely into covenantal relationships with sister churches. In its covenantal relationships the church expresses a realization of both its individual integrity and its fundamental sense of inter-dependence, its contribution to and reliance on the wider Christian community. The capacity to join with other churches in meeting the needs and aspirations of its members, local area, and the wider human community is an important signal of viability.

*Interpersonal fellowship* is the heartbeat of the congregation. Leadership is no less essential for achieving this goal than for achieving institutional viability. The conditions for fellowship include the number and quality of relationships among people in the congregation, the forms in which these relationships are expressed, and the ways by which the entire congregation is experienced as a community. If persons develop their potentialities in relationship with others and if relationships in our society are generally limited to narrow functions in various subgroupings, then the church must be that fellowship in which a wide range of interpersonal relationships can flower around a wide range of perceptions and experiences. Paradoxically, here the small church often misses its opportunity. Among people in a small community who have known one another for a long period, church life tends to be constrained to narrow associational patterns. Moreover, congregational patterns emerging from a former time and now centered in limited age or socioeconomic groupings inhibit new participants. The period of relative autonomy during which new members find their niche is often not well protected in small congregations. It may be, however, that as the steady pace of urbanization changes the character of rural areas, churches will be called upon to play a more vital role in creating conditions for meaningful interpersonal relations and personal fulfillment.

*Stature in the community* at large is the third goal for small churches. Stature implies maturity, influence, and presence, not necessarily size or wealth. A church with stature develops a range of involvement in public concerns and a scale of organizational life appropriate for its mission in the larger community. The church is recognized as an organic community institution, making important contributions to the quality of community life from its particular biblical perspective. A church with stature is an institutional witness to believers and unbelievers. It develops stature through the personal participation of its members in other community organizations and decision-making bodies, through its programs of discussion and projects of community action, and through a highly developed sense of mission among its members which is congruent with the expectations of community leaders. While a community-centered church will always exhibit stature, a church with stature will always, in subtle if not explicit ways, be community oriented.


### Denominational Intervention and the Small Church

Given this perspective on small-church development, what is the role of a denominational agency? Often the denomination is perceived as orienting its programs and resources to the larger and more substantial churches. There is truth in this perception; many denominational resources assume an organizational structure and level of sophistication found more typically in larger churches, and inadequate attention is given to translating programs to smaller situations. But does this perception go to the heart of the matter? Would small-church problems be resolved if a church of one hundred fifty members were seen as the norm for denominational resources? The answers to questions of small-church development go far beyond this kind of solution, important as it is for creating effective program resources. A more fundamental problem is how denominational agencies can help create conditions under which maximum institutional viability, interpersonal fellowship, and community stature can be achieved.

Creating such conditions requires formulating specific policies, staff intervention, research, action planning, and leadership training.

Within most denominations, the middle judicatory (conference, diocese, synod, and so on) is the point at which policies regarding church development are most effective. While middle judicatories are typically limited in the extent to which they can initiate changes in established churches, they are in a position to evaluate the locations of churches and their leadership needs vis-à-vis changing conditions. While most judicatory leaders have a wealth of intuitive knowledge about specific church and community situations, they are often without adequate information for long-range planning and deciding among various options. If judicatories were formally to adopt explicit policies—for example, in terms of the goals outlined above—in lieu of maintaining traditional assumptions, staff activity could more easily be evaluated and focused. In turn, national agencies would have more adequate guidelines for staff and program resource provision.

Policies are different from goals. It is fashionable today for judicatories to adopt goals of 10 to 15 percent increases in church membership without considering whether they are realistic or how they might be achieved. A policy, on the other hand, is an overview statement about the kind of churches which should be projected in given areas and the quality of resources which should be brought to the situations over a specific time period. Policy making requires strategic and ethical decisions, which is probably why it is avoided when possible. A decision must be made to concentrate scarce resources and energy on certain churches. Because of their profound implications, such decisions need to be open and well informed. Examples of judicatory policies might be that five specific churches, because of their strategic locations, would be helped to strengthen their viability factors, three other churches would be helped to increase their community stature, while four churches would be helped to expand their fellowships on the basis of new populations in their areas. Another policy decision might be that instead of investing five thousand dollars a year in each of four separate congregations for a three-year period, twenty thousand dollars a year would be invested in a specialized area minister to work with fifteen congregations. Sound judicatory policies are essential for efficient use of scarce resources.

Intervention with congregations on the basis of judicatory policy should begin prior to policy formulation; local church representatives should have access to the process of policy formulation. Policy implications should be worked out with the congregations in a step-by-step process by the same judicatory representative. The representative may be a staff person, a special project worker, or a neighboring pastor who is recognized as a primary denominational liaison. In any event, the intervener becomes an important part of the church's life over time. He or she is an inside-outsider who works on behalf of the congregation, with perspectives and resources drawn from the larger church, and on behalf of the denomination, with perspectives and resources drawn from the local congregations.

Typically, the intervener will meet first with the pastor, then with the pastor and selected lay leaders, the church board, and other decision-making groups. Within six months, everyone in the church's active membership will know him or her and will be aware of the general policies under which they are working. If the intervener has not gained wide acceptance within six months, there is probably little that can be accomplished through extending the relationship.

One of the key tasks of the intervener is institutional analysis,[2] bringing to awareness some of the objective conditions of the church's organization, membership, and environment, and in so doing raising questions about assumptions which may no longer be realistic for the church. Thus, the intervener works at both the organic and the associative levels of church life. Such work requires a combination of technique and intuition, as well as the ability to elicit and communicate insights that clarify and give direction to the congregation's future.

The intervener brings two interrelated subjective qualities to bear on the congregations. One is leadership style, and the other is a basic way of perceiving the church. Clergy leadership styles can be characterized, in part, with three archtypical attitudes. One is control: The pastor perceives the congregation as a group requiring control and direction; pastoral activity is calculated to manifest control whether through authoritarian, manipulative, or group-process techniques. A second attitude is that of gaining acceptance: The pastor perceives the congregation as a group whose acceptance must constantly be won; pastoral activity is calculated to win admiration and acceptance. A third attitude is that of mutual nonintervention: The pastor perceives the congregation as an alien group with whom one must work for a temporary period; pastoral activity is calculated to avoid activities or relationships which might be construed as leading to more permanent arrangements.

A small church might be perceived more properly as a group of people who, like characters in a drama, are destined to write their own scenarios within a given range of possibilities. They will not be controlled, but they seek direction for living out the best possible scenario instead of muddling through whatever happens to occur. An intervener who has caught his perception of the small church has the dual task of communicating it to both congregation and pastor without becoming a pastor surrogate. An effective intervener thus develops a sense of the congregation's possibilities and limitations from both the inside and the outside.

The United Church of Christ's Board for Homeland Ministries' Small Church Project has developed an intervention strategy of employing full-time project directors in areas containing fifteen to eighteen churches and part-time directors for groups of two to four churches. Each director followed an explicit step-by-step procedure of initiating a covenant relationship with each church and planning with individual churches, sets of churches, and the churches of the entire area. The results of this careful and close attention are a new sense of expectation and potential within the churches, serious attention by their leaders to the realities of institutional life, new relationships among the churches and their leaders, and an openness to change that will enable the churches to chart their way into the future.

On the basis of project results thus far, it is clear that active, systematic planning with churches is most effective at the subconference level. Such planning requires a degree of sustained attention over a period of time that is not efficient on a single-church basis and not feasible on a conference-wide basis. Moreover, the future of a congregation may be related closely to the future of sister congregations. A planning process that includes all potentially relevant combinations of churches is the most flexible and efficient use of resources in the long run. The project director is key at this level as one who models relationships with congregations both for conference staff persons and for local pastors. The director's intervention within the context of national and conference policies becomes the most critical action for bringing about change.

The initial technique employed by the project directors is congregational research derived from the United Church of Christ's Board for Home Ministries' Church Typology Project.[3] Essentially, the intervener collects information about the congregation's membership through a Church Member Inventory administered during one Sunday service, census data, community information, and program information from interviews with the pastor and key laypeople. Research results are then interpreted to church decision-makers. What becomes important is not simply the data that are gathered, but the way in which they stimulate problem definition and new thinking about solutions among church leaders. At this point the insights and intuitions generated by the research process need to be articulated and refined with the help of the intervener. Where there is insight, there is motivation for positive change.

Research interpretation is the opening for action planning, which I shall also refer to as correlational planning. Correlational planning can follow any adequate planning process outline; its distinction lies in style and goal. The goal is to revitalize both the organic and the associational aspects of church life through the structural and procedural means at hand. The style is one which elicits the content of change from the relationship between director and church, circumscribed by the environment, conference policy, the collected data, and the interpersonal character of the congregation as manifest in the relationship.

The major elements of the correlational planning style include:

*Modifying the internal decision-making organization of the church.* Planning for change is usually hampered by decision-making processes geared to stability and tradition. A separate planning committee, on the other hand, often plans in a power vacuum. A planning process of a year or longer requires that responsibility for new thinking be taken by several church groups and correlated. Various options for program, community relationships, and budget resources can be given close attention by different groups, and the results communicated to other groups. The result should be that all church decision-making becomes as inclusive and future oriented as possible.

*Maintaining resource flow to the congregation and its decision-making groups.* Resources include relevant information, examples from the wider church, and, perhaps most important, personal contacts with interested persons outside the congregation. Local community leaders who care about the relevance and future of the church should be heard by the congregation. Neighboring church leaders need to become known, and dialogue between churches established. A well-developed resource flow will be neither too little nor too much for effective group planning; it will provide information and relationships with key people and stimulate new ideas among church leaders.

*Continual clarifying, summarizing, and projecting of new alternatives.* The assumption behind correlational planning is that an active planning process does not determine change but generates it. The church as association requires explicit consent at the basic level for any proposed change. This means that clear democratic procedures must be followed. Both procedures and content are refined through test votes on general issues throughout the planning period. Just as the votes affect immediate church operations, so the modified operations affect future votes. The church as an organic body requires continual nurturing of intersubjective relationships in relation to explicitly determined changes. The explicit and the implicit cannot be conflated into a generalized consensus. Such a foggy practice, while appearing to generate quick support, lends itself to manipulation and to misunderstanding, subverting the long-range associational and organic potential of the church.

Finally, the activity of planning and the experience of change necessarily affect power relationships, and in a small church power is closely tied to personality. What may be most salutary for a person's sense of self-worth may be least so for the congregation's health. Great care must be taken with members whose self-esteem has long been associated with their place in the church. But in most situations, if positive change is to occur, some roles must be made less powerful, others enhanced, and relationships modified. Generally, the long-term benefits of a revitalized congregation are worth short-term dislocations and the anxiety they generate. Here the sensitive denominational intervener can play an invaluable role.

If professional leadership is a key to church development, how is it developed? It is widely noted that seminary training, for all its benefits, does not always provide adequate skills for nurturing churches through periods of substantial change. Part of the answer harks back to the issue of expectations. If career development is not to consist of advancement to bigger and richer churches, what are the alternate satisfactions of vocational achievement? Creating churches that approximate conference policies and receiving psychic and material rewards commensurate with such delicate work are professional satisfactions. Developing serious and constructive peer relationships and contributing to the thought and work of the wider church are professional rewards that need further encouragement and organization. On-the-job training that goes beyond the narrow bounds of organizational development, or other technique-oriented training, and incorporates awareness of people's needs and aspirations combined with the richness of the biblical heritage is what a denomination must provide for its overworked and under-estimated professional leaders.

Here again the middle judicatory is the key unit. Policy formation and the training of leadership to implement policy fall naturally into its purview. Standards for income and recognition for achievement should be part of every judicatory operation. In addition, a clergy training-procedure including every pastor from particular church types in at least three events annually on either a judicatory or a subjudicatory basis would begin to address needs of the clergy. Training should rotate among the disciplines of theological dialogue, social/institutional analysis, and practical technique. Methods should include a combination of recognized expertise, solid reading, and face-to-face encounter. Pastors of small congregations probably need more collegial stimulation but experience less than those in large churches. Because they are prevented from enjoying such encounters by their self-images, their attitudes about long-term church relationships, and lack of respect for others in a similar situation, judicatory intervention and initiation is essential. Finally, pastors in subjudicatory situations where a denominational intervener is at work enjoy the benefits of on-the-job training all year long.

Size is important for church survival, not in itself, but as it affects viability, fellowship, and stature. If big is not beautiful, tiny is not always functional. Small churches are here to stay—if we learn to nurture their potential for witnessing to the spirit of the biblical word. The task of the denomination therefore is not constructing bureaucratic support systems for a class of churches labeled "small," nor is it acting as cheerleader, projecting positive but unrealistic goals. It is the more serious task of collaborating with churches and mutually designing and evolving organic associations of faith which can meet the needs of a society characterized by increasing religious pluralism, moral reassessment, and structural hegemony. Concentrated and selective attention to the institutional transformation of small churches is a major component of this larger task.

## NOTES

1. W. Widdick Schroeder, "Age Cohorts, The Family Life Cycle, and Participation in the Voluntary Church in America: Implications for Membership Patterns—1950–2000." *The Chicago Theological Seminary Register* 65, no. 3 (1975):13–28.

2. Max Stackhouse, "Voluntary Associations and Social Change," *New Conversations* 1, no. 1 (1975):14–23.

3. Theodore H. Erickson and William J. McKinney, "Congregational Typology Construction and Planning for Religious Systems," mimeographed (United Church Board for Homeland Ministries, 1975).